Public Offerings

Stories from the Front Lines
of Community Ministry

Linda-Marie Delloff

Foreword by Martin E. Marty

AN ALBAN INSTITUTE PUBLICATION

Scripture quotations, unless otherwise noted, are from the New Revised Standard Version of the Bible, copyright © 1989, Division of Christian Education of the National Council of Churches in the United States of America, and are used with permission.

This book was written with the support of Lilly Endowment Inc.

Library of Congress Card Number 2002109029

ISBN 1-56699-268-0

> *"The reason we exist as a church*
> *is for the sake of those who aren't here."*

> — The Reverend John Bent
> Christ Lutheran Church
> Whitefish, Montana

Contents

As I read Linda-Marie Delloff's memorable chapters, I kept asking: "Why doesn't every congregation do what those described here do—contribute boldly and effectively to the public or publics in which they find themselves?" What makes these ten congregations exemplary? They exist in many different kinds of circumstances, so we cannot say they all do excellent public ministry because they are all big, or urban, or suburban, or Jewish, or rich, or poor. No, the answer has to come from somewhere else.

Jose Ortega y Gasset, the Spanish philosopher, had as his life motto—call it observation more than motto—"I am I and my circumstances." You do not have to be an expert on foreign languages to get the point of what "circumstances" are. Circum = around. Stance = stance! The individual is a combination of herself and the circumstances—the people and places—among which she finds herself.

No, Ortega elaborated: "If I do not save my circumstances, I do not save myself." The congregations described in this book have looked around themselves, and they have realized that to save themselves, they must save their surrounding circumstances and the people—the publics—who both create and reflect the circumstances.

Through the years I've been moved by the "creative selfishness" of Jeremiah 29 in the Bible. God's people are in exile. They would best be described as a confused, low-morale, directionless congregation. Why? Among other things, they were so because they did not look at *what was around them*. They did not study their circumstances or the heterogeneous publics among which their own homogeneous congregation was living. Instead, they escaped through nostalgia into a past that had never been quite as golden as it now appeared.

They escaped through envisioning what it would be like to return to Jerusalem and build the temple.

Both what they looked back on and forward to had qualities worth developing. But they could not do what the Lord called them to do at the present time because they did not *look around and outside themselves*. The "letter" that Jeremiah reads them tells them precisely to look at and "save" their circumstances: "Seek the welfare of the city where I have sent you, . . . for in its welfare you will find your welfare" (v. 7).

Further, merely to *notice* the circumstance is not enough. The believer can take Ortega's theme and carry it away. He did not say, "I am I." That would mean solipsism, selfishness, living enclosed in a hall of mirrors. He did not say, "I am my circumstances." That would have been fatalism, passivity, stupefaction. No, he wanted a dialogue *between* self and environ. There illumination begins.

Read about these congregations and

notice what they noticed: that they are publics in public. They realize needs distinctive to their place and time and then draw on theological resources of their particular traditions. George Santayana says that we do not speak "language," we speak "Korean" or "Spanish." So we do not observe "religion," we practice Judaism or Mennonitism. Santayana says that it is the surprising, sometimes idiosyncratic, particular, peculiar stories of a tradition (concentrated here in a local community) that give it saving power. As you read these stories, ask yourself, Who within each congregation had the vision to notice the circumstances? Who decided to do something about it? What theological motives and motifs seemed to empower each group?

Catholicism has a teaching called "subsidiarity." It's a safeguard against indifference or apathy caused by the experience that bureaucracies are remote and complex. It's a push to begin where one is. Decisions and responses

> These congregations forge ahead to deal with and "save" some aspect of their circumstances, whether one block away or a globe away.

should be on the "lowest," most local level. Of course, the congregations in these stories are linked—to other congregations, to jurisdictions, to public and private agencies. But they do not wait for others to act. They forge ahead to deal with and "save" some aspect of their circumstances, whether one block away or a globe away.

And Delloff says they do this "saving" in unusually creative ways, "cutting-edge" ways. The latter phrase can be a cliché unless handled and developed with care, as Delloff does. Just what does it mean? What is "cutting-edge" public ministry? What do these congregations "cut?" What is at the "edge?" What is the result of their "cutting?" Let me warn you that I am

ix

going to resort to a kind of medieval pun, some serious wordplay.

A word that appears frequently in Delloff's introductory chapters is *example*, as in "for example" and "examples" and "learning by example." Each of the narrative chapters itself is "an example." What is an example? In the Middle Ages a Latin lexicon would have directed the curious word-searcher to *exemplum*. Even a blah dictionary for collegians today will identify the word *example* as having derived from *eximere*, to "take out." In olden days, more imaginative lexicographers reminded us that *exemplum* then referred to that which is cut out, and, most notably and precisely, an *exemplum* was a "clearing in the woods."

The internal life of a congregation and the circumstances of its environment can be foreboding at worst and confusing at best. Anyone lost in thick woods knows that she is in a tangle, a bramble, a pathless, trackless situation. And then, voilà, an *exemplum* appears. It makes clear: Here the woods end. Here a new space begins. Here you can get perspective and refind your way.

Also, there is the matter of "light." Pathless, trackless woods are bad enough when sun breaks through in broad daylight. When night falls or when the canopy of branches and leaves is so thick as to block out the sky, it is easy to stumble, to get lost, to become a victim. Then, in the distance is a brighter spot. You break through and find that you are in a clearing in the woods. An *exemplum*.

Congregations today need all the light they can receive. I picture all ten of these congregational clearings, these *exempla*, as being of service to people who are not in the precise situations of any of them. Some urban congregations may very well find light shine on their ways by rural ministries in this book, and vice versa.

Linda-Marie Delloff is a reliable and articulate guide who, without any condescension, not in any overbearing tutorial manner, leads readers on visits to these hospitable places, these congregations that are engaging with their publics in dynamic and creative ways. She may stop and point, here and there, to something for our instruction. In most cases, she simply and clearly tells the stories of the places that by their nature are *exempla* and, therefore, of service to all who would see.

Dr. Delloff and the Alban Institute pass the stories on to others, hoping that they will be moved to look outside themselves, to add their own stories about their own circumstances and publics: how to "save" them and thus themselves and what they hold dear.

MARTIN E. MARTY

This volume is something of a departure for the Alban Institute. Many Alban publications are manuals; that is, they provide specific steps for how a congregation might accomplish a particular goal. In contrast, this is a book of stories. There is no system or theory explained here, though the introduction does provide some generalizations. The stories certainly make points, but they are made by example rather than by instruction. The people making those points are not "experts" in community ministry. Rather, they are members and clergy of local congregations who are amazingly creative in developing fresh ways of meeting community challenges within their own context.

There is nothing new about public ministry. But there are always new ways of doing it and new areas of need. The Alban Institute was curious about recent developments in how congregations relate to the many communities they serve. Research to undertake that project was generously funded by a grant from Lilly Endowment, Inc. To that institution go thanks, as well as to the congregations who so generously welcomed a researcher to spend some time visiting and pulling members away from their ministries in order to ask questions and probe the whys and hows of what they are doing.

It was difficult to select the small number of congregations described here, and many people helped in suggesting choices. There are countless examples of new developments in public ministry around the country. The ways in which these congregations function do not encompass all approaches to community service. Rather, they are representative of the wide and rich variety being exemplified daily in churches and synagogues everywhere. Sometimes religious congregations do not receive adequate public credit for the public work they do. In addition to providing examples that might inspire other congregations to act, this and other studies attempt to redress that inadequacy—to call public attention to public ministry.

This collection of narratives describes Christian and Jewish congregations in the United States that are currently conducting "cutting-edge public ministry." Congregations of most faiths have always been involved in "public ministry"— that is, service with persons beyond the congregation's membership or regular participants. By definition, to live one's religion in the midst of the world includes a public component. Different faiths and denominations emphasize public involvement to greater or lesser degree, however, and the word *public* can have different meanings for different groups. The stories here portray many, though by no means all, levels of public involvement and definitions of *public*.

The book tells 10 stories, six of them in considerable detail, each comprising a chapter. The final chapter contains four shorter stories about exceptional public ministry in the New York City area following the World Trade Center disaster of September 11, 2001. The 10 case studies:

- Alfred Street Baptist Church (Progressive National Baptist Convention), Alexandria, Virginia. *Notable for:* The all-encompassing penetration of public ministry into every aspect of church life and the sophistication of its organizational methods.

- Christ Lutheran Church, (Evangelical Lutheran Church in America), Whitefish, Montana. *Notable for:* Shepherd's Hand Clinic, serving people who have no medical insurance.

- Grace Episcopal Church, Nutley, New Jersey. *Notable for:* Post-September 11 ministry with families of Americans serving in the armed forces.

- Holy Cross/Immaculate Heart of Mary Roman Catholic Parish, Chicago, Illinois. *Notable for:* Dugan Alternative High School, serving drop-outs and other troubled youth.

- Judson Memorial Church (American Baptist and United Church of Christ), New York City. *Notable for:* Hosting public ministry with people unemployed as a result of September 11.

- Kehillat Israel Synagogue (Reconstructionist), Pacific Palisades, California. *Notable for:* Overall emphasis on public service and unique approach to encouraging social commitment among members.

- Oakhurst Presbyterian Church (Presbyterian Church in the U.S.A.), Decatur, Georgia.

2

Notable for: Training members and others to be public advocates and lobbyists for governmental legislation.

- Congregation Ohab Zedek (Orthodox Jewish), New York City.
  Notable for: Ongoing vigil for bodies of September 11 victims.

- St. Andrew's Episcopal Church, Denver, Colorado.
  Notable for: The Children's Center for Arts and Learning.

- Saint Peter's Lutheran Church (Evangelical Lutheran Church in America), New York City.
  Notable for: Its role as a "public church" following September 11 events.

These stories primarily use the term public ministry rather than, for example, social ministry or outreach. This choice resides in an effort to describe programs that go beyond serving the most basic social needs such as food and shelter. One of the case studies focuses on the arts and art history, for instance; another includes teaching parenting skills; a third involves government lobbying. These examples do not fall automatically into the category of social ministry as it has been traditionally understood. However, some Jewish congregations would not use the term ministry at all. They are more comfortable with phrases such as outreach program, so that and other alternative terms also appear.

Cutting-edge refers to what is newest and most creative among the thousands of vital outreach ministries through which congregations are helping to solve problems. In some cases, cutting-edge means keeping up with urgent and obvious new needs, such as providing medical care to people without insurance, or dealing with unemployment resulting from the Trade Center disasters in New York City.

A congregation can have and serve several different publics, defined geographically or by their characteristics.

In other cases, congregations go out and look for new types of outreach, probing beneath the surface to reveal less obvious issues whose amelioration would significantly improve the lives of particular groups of people. One such example is the food program of Alfred Street Baptist Church in Alexandria, Virginia, whose participants learned through experience that many homeless people avoid shelters and so would not benefit from food taken there. They further realized that the hungry people they were targeting needed visiting and conversation as well as food and clothing. So they designed their food delivery program to include stops at public parks, and they built time for visiting into the delivery schedule.

A congregation can have and serve several different publics. It is possible to define such publics geographically—for instance, the congregation's immediate neighborhood, its town, a surrounding metropolitan area, "the rural south," an area of Latin America. Or a congregation may define a public by its characteristics, such as "homeless adults," or "deaf people," or "children who have trouble communicating." A public may include both descriptives, as in "homeless adults in our immediate neighborhood." A congregation may identify several different publics whom it wants to serve. This identification process will depend on factors such as the congregation's location, size, ages of members, and availability of resources—both human and financial. It will also depend on whether the congregation feels it has a good chance of being successful with a particular ministry.

Other factors, such as affinities within the congregation, may figure into the equation. A congregation that includes a number of African immigrants might identify an important public it wants to serve in Africa. Or somewhat the opposite may obtain: a homogeneous, European American congregation may decide that it is important to expand its experience by serving an ethnically mixed group of people in a nearby city. A congregation of a particular denomination could decide that an important part of its public is members of the same denomination who live in other parts of the world. There are myriad possibilities and combinations for a congregation defining its publics.

Public ministries can be primarily "inside" or "outside" programs. In the first case the congregation's building is home to the ministry, such as a place for homeless people to sleep, a clothing distribution center, or a tutoring program. Some inside activities are "ministries of hospitality" that allow groups not associated with the congregation to use its space for their own needs. Many congregations offer this type of hospitality in addition to whatever

additional public ministries they operate. An "outside" program takes place away from the building: in city parks, or on the streets where youth gather, or in a hospital. A congregation may combine the two types in one program. For example, Holy Cross/Immaculate Heart of Mary Roman Catholic Parish in Chicago sponsors an alternative school that meets in its buildings, but some of the services provided to students, such as job training or placement, occur in other settings. Most congregations involved in public ministry support more than one outreach program, and are accustomed to moving around, both within the building and outside it.

It is probably safe to say that most congregations wish to serve the public, or an element of it, in some way. Yet many simply do not know how. They do

---

Most congregations wish to serve the public in some way, but many simply do not know how.

5

not know how to assess need, how to choose a project, how to set it up, or how to carry it out. They may not know what skills and talents their members have and could use in developing the capacity for public ministry, or what kinds of resources a particular project would require. Such challenges and details can easily overwhelm a sincere interest and discourage a congregation from proceeding. The congregations described here have negotiated these questions successfully, and their results are distinguished by being cutting edge in content or methodology.

Distinctive Examples

Two basic questions guided the search for these stories. First, What kinds of new or unusual programs are American congregations currently conducting? And second, How have these congregations developed the capacity to do so effectively? Creativity can be expressed in the particular type of public ministry, in the way that ministry is conducted— or both.

The stories in this book include unusual offerings such as the comprehensive arts/art history program, a support group for loved ones of military personnel, and a summer camp for children in war-torn areas. Other congregations offer more traditional types of ministries, such as feeding the homeless or providing shelter, but employ fresh and creative means to do so, such as teaching congregation members how to do public lobbying, or making a "change the world" pledge a key part of worship on important holy days. Often, because of its overall creativity and its dedication to exploring the new, a congregation will be cutting edge in both the content and the methods of its public ministries.

The narratives address such questions as these: How and why does a congregation decide to undertake public ministry? What are the steps involved in developing the capacity to do so? Are these steps the same in every case? Is there a "formula"? One of the most basic issues this book examines is how public ministries relate to other aspects of congregational life. How do they grow out of particular theological convictions? How do they relate to worship? How does a congregation decide who within the membership will be involved in public ministry? Will it be an outreach committee? Or is there some way that public ministry can cut across all aspects of what the congregation believes and does?

What This Book Is Not

This is not a book about "charitable choice," though the issue is relevant. The term refers to legislation, first passed in 1996, that encourages faith-based organizations to use government money to shoulder more of the nation's social burden. The interest in congregations' public ministries has grown in the atmosphere percolating around this legislation and gained new impetus after the election of President George W. Bush, who created a new entity, the White House Office of Faith-Based and Community Initiatives, to deal with the issue. All of the congregations described here, however, became involved because of their own theological convictions rather than as a result of government admonition or legislative encouragement.

Neither is this a book about evangelization—going into the public primarily in order to attract new members. The ministries described here, especially those that take place away from the congregation's meeting place, often occur without the recipients knowing that a religious congregation is responsible. Even if someone passing out food is wearing a clerical collar, for example, recipients won't know what group the clergyperson represents unless they ask. Without exception, these congregations take great pains to avoid

> Though successful public ministries have many elements in common, there is no "one right way" to conduct such programs; every succeess is a story unto itself.

the appearance of proselytizing. Often they work among groups of people who either belong to another faith or to none, or of whose religious beliefs they know nothing, and of whose feelings they are scrupulously respectful. Certainly this is not the case with all congregations' public ministries, but it is true about those described here.

Nor is this book a manual of instructions. Rather, it illustrates points or suggests ideas by telling stories. There are definite reasons for this approach. Though successful public ministries have many elements in common, there is no "one right way" to conduct such programs; every success is a story unto itself. Even the common features are best illustrated through stories of the ministries rather than by merely listing a set of steps their organizers have identified as working well. Further, every story is more than the sum of its parts, that is, more than a list of decisions and actions. It is in that overall sum that the real identity of any congregation is to be found.

This grouping of congregations has no presumption of being comprehensive; these are but a handful, a small sampling of the thousands engaged in outstanding public ministry. Similarly, a reader should not expect to identify his or her congregation as obviously one or another "type" depicted in the book. Rather, these examples are representative, and a reader may find traits of his or her own congregation in several of the examples.

The traits cut across the sample congregations as well. For instance, in terms of content or method of public ministry, a medium-sized suburban congregation might happen to have more in common with a small rural church than with another suburban congregation. It is important to consider all of the elements cited in the examples, and to realize that the combinations may change or evolve.

As noted, the stories are intended to be suggestive rather than instructive. Thus, they avoid strict categorization and labeling. Rather, the aim is to encourage creative thinking "across categories." One reason for this approach is to deter a congregation from deciding that, because it does not have exactly the same traits as one of those featured here, it cannot be successful in doing public ministry.

CHAPTER 1

GOING PUBLIC

What Is a "Public"?

I n serving God, whom within the world, beyond its own membership, does a congregation serve? Answering this question must become a self-conscious and deliberate process for every congregation. But even prior to asking this question, it is vital for a congregation to define who it is and what its mission is. If members are vague on those two questions, they will be even vaguer in understanding whom that mission is designed to serve. A variety of resources exist for helping congregations conduct such basic explorations and articulate basic self-definitions, such as *Studying Congregations: A New Handbook*, edited by Nancy T. Ammerman et al. (more helpful titles are listed in the Selected Resources section of this book).

11

> Only after a congregation
> is certain of its own identity
> can it confidently hope
> to determine appropriate ways
> of serving the larger public.

All of the congregations described here are keenly aware of who they are, and secure in that knowledge. They operate out of that knowledge, and everything they do is a conscious reflection of it. They have each arrived at their definitions by somewhat different means, over varying lengths of time, but all have made systematic, determined efforts to reach that goal. For example, Saint Peter's Lutheran Church in New York City posts its mission statement around the church and on its Web site, and constantly refers to it when considering new ministry.

Only after a congregation is certain of its own identity can it confidently hope to determine appropriate ways of serving the larger public. As in defining mission and identity, the process of selecting a public(s) has been deliberate for each of the sample congregations. Certainly in a crisis a congregation may respond instinctively and without making such distinctions. But over the long run, a congregation needs carefully and corporately to decide whom it wants to and can serve best.

The process of identification and definition can happen in two ways. In the first a need becomes obvious, and then its population is identified. For example, a congregation might say, "We know that our town has food services for hungry people but no counseling and training services to help them get on their feet. Could we undertake such a program? How many people need these services? How do we find them? And do we actually have the means to serve them?" Members of Grace Episcopal Church in Nutley, New Jersey were aware that the armed services run spiritual support groups for military personnel, but realized there were no such groups for their families and loved ones.

In the other case, a congregation may first identify a specific public—perhaps those living in its neighborhood—and then ask, "What are their needs?" For instance, a common situation involves an older urban congregation that notices its neighborhood is changing and is now home mostly to recent immigrants. The congregation may then decide to find out what needs those recent residents have and do its best to meet one or more of them.

As the stories will reveal, a crucial component of public ministry is to limit a congregation's currently served publics to those it can logically expect to serve effectively. Even the largest congregation, or one with many resources, will have to limit its ministries in order to carry them out efficiently. That is one of the reasons for highlighting a representative variety of congregations: urban, suburban, and rural; large and small; wealthy and those of modest means. In this regard, too, there is much crossover among types, and categories are never rigid.

Similarities among Successful Public Ministries

Congregations successful in public ministry exhibit a number of similarities. While avoiding neat categorizations, it is nonetheless helpful to make some broad generalizations. The following discussion of 11 similarities divides into two sections: (1) traits that deal primarily with *developing the capacity* to do cutting-edge public ministry, and (2) traits that apply to ministries that are up and running smoothly.

This list of commonalties is not exhaustive. Nor does every congregation cited possess all of these traits. These broad generalizations definitely have exceptions.

> Congregations are willing,
> even eager, to accept these risks
> because they know that
> by always being "safe,"
> they will never change anything.

Developing the Capacity

Congregations that are good at public ministry almost always incorporate the following steps into developing the capacity to carry out a ministry.

1. Such congregations recognize, then overcome their fears, or at least they are *willing to take risks despite their fears*. These fears may include failure, rejection by the targeted public, physical or emotional discomfort, even physical danger. They can also be fears of "the other," that is, of people who are very different from oneself. Such congregations are willing, even eager, to accept these risks because they know that by always being "safe," they will never change anything.

   They make processing the fears an early and distinct part of the preparation process for any new ministry. Of course, new fears and problems may emerge later, but with a process of discussion and acknowledgment in place, participants are readily able to deal with setbacks and unforeseen worries.

2. Successful public ministries usually originate with a strong "*idea person*," someone who is "inspired" to initiate discussion of a new program. Often the idea will be connected to something in that person's experience or background. An example is the Rev. Connie Delzell at St. Andrew's Episcopal Church in Denver, whose idea for a children's arts ministry began with her own daughter's childhood experience. Another is the medical

ministry at Christ Lutheran Church in Whitefish, Montana, where two medical professionals became aware through their work of a crucial need for free medical services in the area.

An idea may also derive from a person's experience in somewhat the opposite way. For instance, a member of Kehillat Israel Synagogue in California developed a passion for feeding the hungry not because he himself had ever lacked food. Quite the opposite. Keenly aware of his plenitude of blessings, he felt a strong need to serve those with less. The idea person may be clergy or lay but will always be someone who truly burns with a fervor to address a particular need.

This factor may differ according to faith group. For example, in Judaism and Roman Catholicism clergy generally play a stronger role in this regard, though in both cases laypeople are assuming more

leadership. The latter has been true of Protestantism, especially liberal Protestantism, for some time. There, laypeople may be even more apt to take the initiative in introducing a new idea to the congregation. However, neither of these tendencies is true in all cases.

3. A consciously established *atmosphere of encouragement* makes it possible for a member to comfortably introduce an idea about his or deepest passion is. Congregations who do good public ministry generally convey the attitude that, at least initially, "We'll consider any idea." Congregational leaders constantly work to ensure a conducive atmosphere for ideas to

---

Congregations who do good public ministry generally convey the attitude that, "We'll consider any idea."

---

emerge from anyone at just about any time.

Ideas don't have to come from a congregational leader, and there is more than one forum in which members may freely voice their own. This variety includes meetings of various committees; adult discussion groups; seemingly unrelated groups like Bible study; social occasions. Systematic examination of an idea follows, but successful public-ministry congregations encourage openness and broadly based enthusiasm for new ideas.

4. Congregations with healthy outreach programs take care to *identify the gifts, skills, and special interests* of members before beginning any new ministry. Exploration of members' individual traits usually goes beyond a standard "time and talent survey," includes more detail, and has planned follow-up that includes regular phone calls and personal contact by leaders. Leaders make sure that the right people are in the right groups.

If people don't volunteer, leaders encourage them to an appropriate degree, though they don't apply uncomfortable pressure. As a deacon at Alfred Street Baptist Church in Alexandria, Virginia explains, "We don't push, we lead." Leaders realize that, in addition to interest and talent, personality is important, too. For example, someone might be knowledgeable about a topic but not be an outgoing "people person" and would feel ill at ease in certain situations.

For other reasons, too, expertise does not always decree that a person pursue a particular ministry. Some might want to get away from what they do professionally. An accountant might rather be on the buildings and grounds committee than help with a project budget.

These congregations differ in the degree to which they express *expectations* that members participate in public ministry, and that their personal skills are a gift to be shared in that service. A thoughtful congregation works to balance all these factors.

Congregations skilled at public ministry also recognize that one member's passion might be of much less interest to everyone else. In addition to looking at the practical aspects of a potential program, leaders make sure that the whole congregation has an opportunity to respond fully to the idea. Even though a small group might be willing to do all the work, the best public ministries have an entire congregation behind them.

5. While every public ministry described here originated in someone's passion, congregation members quickly worked it into a

The best public ministries have an entire congregation behind them.

practical plan. Passion is primary, but it cannot run a program. Participants squarely face such nitty-gritty issues as raising and sustaining funds, finding appropriate personnel and volunteers to carry out a ministry, and making sure they address the long-term as well as the short-term challenges.

A congregation conducting a successful public ministry includes people who are energized by the challenge of organization and detail. Such people do not dread forming a comprehensive financial plan, learning how to apply for a grant, or informing themselves about the government regulations that may apply to some programs. They like to work on execution, are patient, and can see if and how the ministry

17

To the degree that a congregation has a prior general plan for reaching to a crisis, the more smoothly any new response will go.

will fit into the congregation's overall life. Maintaining that overall vision is certainly a clergy responsibility, although laypeople share it as well.

Though all successful public ministries eventually work only if they have a comprehensive plan, the initial phase may differ from case to case. At St. Andrew's Episcopal Church in Denver, a big risk and leap came first, followed later by the plan. In contrast, Alfred Street Baptist Church has developed such a high degree of organization that a fairly specific procedure is already in place for investigating possibilities for any new ministry.

Circumstances will also determine the order in which steps occur.

Following the September 11 events in New York City, it was necessary for area congregations to jump feet first into a variety of ministries they may never have tried. This is always true in a crisis. But to the degree that a congregation has a prior general plan for reacting to a crisis, the more smoothly any new response will go. Congregation Ohab Zedek had never conducted a public vigil, but members (for example, serving in an ambulance corps) were trained in crisis response and were already self-conscious about their desire for public service. This previously thought-out readiness facilitated their ability to address the September 11 events.

6. Planners of successful public ministries make sure that, within reasonable limits, *every age group* can help with some aspect of the project. Certainly, frail elderly people cannot tote large containers of food

and clothing to parks to find homeless people, nor can children. But there will be some other activity these groups can undertake: assemble the food perhaps, or fold the clothing, or conduct prayer ministries.

Different age groups may also carry out their own special ministries, but every age group within the congregation is aware of the others, of how it might help out with a particular ministry, and of the significance the congregation accords public ministry in general. Teaching this awareness starts with the congregation's young children. At these congregations, outreach is discussed in Sabbath school programs and other children's activities, using Bible stories and other age-appropriate materials.

At a young age, children begin to participate in public ministry. Alfred Street Baptist Church has a group for mothers and three-year-

olds, where the children begin to learn social concern by interacting with each other. Around age 10 or younger, children visit nursing homes to sing. Kehillat Israel runs a religious school that incorporates projects to foster awareness of social responsibility. In many congregations children make gifts for sick or disadvantaged children or for other people in need.

Ministries That Are Operating Smoothly

The prior list of traits applies to the process of developing capacity for public ministry. The following traits consistently appear in programs that have moved beyond the developmental stage and have been functioning well for some time.

1. *Laypeople lead* all of the public ministries described here. In some

cases, an original idea came from a clergyperson, but developing capacity and management quickly became lay responsibilities. Such an arrangement requires cooperation from both sides; that is, clergy must want laypeople to lead, and laypeople must desire to lead. If either element is missing, chances for success are low.

In some cases, the same people lead a ministry over a long period of time, especially if it requires specialized knowledge like medical or teaching experience. In other cases, leadership may rotate, though in the best situations there is a planned and careful transition from one leader to another. Some

---

The congregation's worship and preaching support the ministry and help to explain why it is important.

---

congregations build capacity for change into the system. In others the structure is less formal but the general communication lines are open enough that more than one person begins to sense when a change would be appropriate.

2. Creative public ministries are interwoven in a variety of ways into *every aspect of congregational life*. They are not simply turned over to a "social action" committee or some other small group. The congregation's worship and preaching support the ministry and help to explain why it is important. This can happen in a number of ways. People who carry out a particular ministry might conduct worship using examples from their experience. Or people served by the ministry might come to deliver a message. At St. Andrew's in Denver, children in the Children's Center for Arts and Learning choir

sing often at Sunday worship. At Alfred Street, every ministry has its own special days for which it plans worship and highlights its work (though such focus is not confined to those days).

Keeping the emphasis consistent and strong is usually overall a clergy responsibility. In preaching, clergy not only highlight the congregation's ministries, but also discuss the specific theological reasons for why public ministry is important. This includes regular references to sacred texts that direct followers to behave in certain ways, along with explanations of what the directions mean.

An example is a Labor Day service at Kehillat Israel, in which the rabbi and cantor used texts and music illustrating the value and importance of meaningful work to an individual's self-esteem. Other speakers described a current project helping non-union laborers organize to obtain better treatment from their employers. At Oakhurst Presbyterian Church in Decatur, Georgia, according to Pastor Nibs Stroupe, "Our worship is formative of who we are, and it sets the style for our public ministry." Members see worship and outreach as inextricably linked.

These congregations plan events around their public ministries. Often these are fundraisers, but not necessarily. They may be purely social events. An example of the latter is a Christmas party at Denver's Children's Center for Arts and Learning. Parishioners help in the planning, prepare and bring food, and attend the party if possible to spend time with the children. A congregation might have a work day when many members show up to prepare materials for a particular ministry. As noted elsewhere, an adult forum or a Bible study group might discuss the ministry and its meaning for that group's members.

3. *Communication* is good in congregations with successful public ministries. As pointed out, all members have a chance to participate in deciding whether to support the ministry. There are congregational meetings just for that purpose. Then those carrying out the ministry regularly inform the congregation about the ministry's operation. This can be through reports and announcements presented at worship or meetings, stories in a newsletter, reports and photos posted on bulletin boards, or a special periodic publication devoted to the ministry. There is opportunity for ongoing feedback from the congregation.

There is also a good deal of informal conversation: for example, at a social hour held after worship, or at a women's group meeting on a weeknight. Leaders in the ministry make sure that every parishioner, whether he or she participates directly, is well informed.

4. Ministries that work for their intended public also *enrich the congregation.* In the programs described here, the results (though not necessarily planned to do so) feed back into the congregation in ways that benefit members, both as individuals and as a community.

At Holy Cross in Chicago, the presence of the high school for troubled youth led to a comprehensive series of parenting classes for parish members. The members of Congregation Ohab Zedek in New York City experienced unexpected new growth and depth in their individual spirituality as a result of taking part in the congregation's vigil for victims of the Trade Center tragedy.

Another byproduct of people working together in a ministry is a heightened sense of community and intimacy among the participants themselves.

Almost always, another by-product of people working together in a ministry is a heightened sense of community and intimacy among the participants themselves. The group at Alfred Street Baptist Church who cook together and then spend most of a day delivering the food have developed an easy camaraderie and a sense of mutual support that extends far beyond the time they spend volunteering.

Other kinds of new relationships also emerge. The congregation as a whole, even a large one, inevitably develops a greater sense of community as participants share stories and information about the public ministries. Congregations may develop new relationships with other groups they meet through their outreach. One of these is obviously the public served by the ministry, but relationships may form with other congregations working toward the same goals, or with stores willing to donate supplies, or with governmental or private groups involved in the work

5. Congregations with effective public ministry *know their own limits*. This factor applies to all of the previously described stages of a public ministry. These limits include resources—financial or other—as well as time and people-power. There are built-in supports for volunteers (such as regular calls from leaders) and various aids to avoid burnout (such as an occasional retreat or time away from the program). Ministry participants may be very busy but they don't seem depleted. They may start a ministry with a big splash but they also know how to moderate and sustain their level of energy. They find ways to renew their enthusiasm, such as taking a workshop or inviting experts to speak to volunteers.

Awareness of limits is especially important when planning a new

23

ministry, but it needs to be revisited as the situation shifts with the ministry or the congregation. For instance, the pool of volunteers may shrink. Or the ministry may grow so much that it is better to spin it off to become self-sustaining than to struggle with insufficient resources to accommodate the growth.

Dugan High School in Chicago limits the number of students who can enroll in its programs. Part of its goal is to offer individual attention to the youth, so the number is restricted. There are also limits of space and capacity. The Whitefish clinic limits cases to those that don't require extensive equipment: the clinic doesn't do surgery, for example, and doesn't have in-struments for sophisticated diagnostic testing. Instead, it has relationships with hospitals to handle such needs. Oakhurst Presbyterian Church in Decatur limits the number of public issues it takes on, primarily because

of clergy and lay time constraints. The Employment Project at Judson Memorial Church in New York City does not actually help people get jobs; it limits its activity to supporting them and educating them about how to do so.

Being aware of limits includes the crucial component of *patience*. It is tempting to want everything to happen all at once, to achieve instant success in solving a problem. But this miracle virtually never happens, and volunteers conducting healthy public ministries constantly remind themselves of that reality. Nor is there really a fixed, identifiable point at which participants can say, "This problem is solved." A tolerance for ambiguity is a valuable asset for doing public ministry.

Awareness of limits, but-tressed by self-conscious patience, applies to a project's results as well as to the timespan required. Congregations differ in the time it takes to develop a well-functioning public ministry. This depends on the congregation's age, size, staff size, resources, and other factors. For instance, the early stages of the Children's Center for Arts and Learning were slow because the church could not afford a staff secretary.

The crucial point is that the congregations described here did not give in to discouragement if events proceeded slowly. Similarly, they were not easily discouraged if something didn't work the first time around. Shepherd's Hand Clinic in Montana had to abandon its first try at dental services, but used the experience to learn how to improve in a later attempt that did achieve its purpose.

❖ ❖ ❖

As congregations change, so too do their ministries. Publics also change. Creative

> **Creative congregations remain flexible and open to fresh ideas for adapting a current ministry to new developments.**

congregations remain flexible and open to fresh ideas for adapting a current ministry to new developments. Finally, they are also open to letting go some or all of the ministry when it no longer seems appropriate or when that congregation no longer seems to be the right sponsor. As expressed by a member of Oakhurst Presbyterian Church, "We don't feel we 'own' any of our ministries." Often the greatest success for a public ministry is when it begins to operate on its own—or when it is no longer needed at all.

CHAPTER 2

FOLLOWING THE VISION

THE CHILDREN'S CENTER FOR ARTS AND LEARNING
ST. ANDREW'S EPISCOPAL CHURCH, DENVER, COLORADO

When Heather Delzell McKay, now in her 30s, was a child, she had considerable trouble in school. Major reading difficulties made her fear all her subjects and dislike school in general. After some time, it was discovered that Heather is dyslexic—a condition which, if ignored, can cause serious problems. But Heather was lucky. The Delzell family had always loved art and music, and offered frequent opportunities for involvement with both. Through the arts, especially painting, Heather found a means of expression that not only made her comfortable; she excelled at it.

Heather became increasingly self-confident and was able to negotiate all her school subjects much more successfully. Today she is a professional artist who teaches part-time at the Denver Art Students League and exhibits her paintings in local galleries.

But her primary job is as director of the Children's Center for Arts and Learning (CCAL), an inner-city Denver neighborhood ministry sponsored by St. Andrew's Episcopal Church, to which she belongs.

Founded in 1993, the Center is the result of divine inspiration—and sheer determination—on the part of McKay's mother, the Reverend Constance Delzell, rector of St. Andrew's. The church was a struggling diocesan mission when Delzell arrived. Parishioners credit her with increasing membership, improving finances, and introducing creative new programming. Delzell (the first Episcopal woman ordained in Colorado) is nothing if not resolute. The skills and dedication leading to St. Andrew's growth were also essential to the success the Center currently enjoys.

Since its opening, the CCAL has moved three times to accommodate the increasing number of children whose parents want them to participate. Currently, between 60 and 85 children,

ages 5 to 12, are enrolled at any given time, and there is always a waiting list. The maximum number of students is determined by space and resources to pay teachers' fees. Some youth have been participating in the program for years. Several have thrived to such a degree that their CCAL experience has shaped their high-school studies and vocational aspirations.

The Reverend Nancee Martin-Coffey has served as the Center's development officer and volunteer coordinator, as well as a St. Andrew's staff member. She points out that in addition to its growth, another mark of the Center's success is that the children begin to perform better in school. Teachers and administrators report that grades go up, the children express more curiosity, and they clearly have a more positive attitude.

The Urban Quandary

St. Andrew's, a small congregation in downtown Denver, is bordered on one side by a pocket of growth and gentrification. On the other side stretches a large area of poverty and its related problems. Though the area, comprised of several neighborhoods, extends far beyond St. Andrew's own immediate vicinity, the congregation regards the whole as its public. The at-risk children there generally have a hard time with school. They have particular trouble learning to read, process information, and express themselves. These challenges are made more difficult by their pervasive lack of self-confidence. Often they don't receive much support or encouragement at home, where there tend to be a variety of problems. The children end up disliking school, failing, perhaps dropping out later, and ultimately minimizing their future opportunities.

As in many urban school systems, Denver has initiated major cuts in programs. One of its money-saving moves was the elimination of music and art from the elementary school curriculum. Because of their previous involvement with the area's children in tutoring groups, the St. Andrew's congregation was well aware of the kids' general difficulties with school, as well as the elimination of the arts from their programs.

Ever since her daughter had found a means of expression and joy through painting, Delzell had thought about helping other children in similar ways. After she had been at St. Andrew's only a short time, she awoke one night from a dream, which she is certain "was sent by God." The dream told her that this was the time and place to take action on her wish to establish an arts ministry. In

It seems that the Center
and the congregation
were mutual spurs to growth
and have blossomed together.

29

this case, one could say that the original vision for a ministry came before identification of the need or a specific public. Delzell had a thought in the back of her head that didn't crystallize until the dream and her recognition of the appropriate public and need.

In fact, it seems that the Center and the congregation were mutual spurs to growth and have blossomed together. The Center provided an additional purpose and was a galvanizing factor in the congregation's early efforts to stabilize. Partly because of its reputation for rich liturgical practice and an excellent choir, St. Andrew's has a number of artists among its members. They became such enthusiasts about Delzell's idea for an arts center that there was little difficulty in convincing the rest of the congregation. Even though the Center quickly grew out of its church space, the congregation has continued to be involved in a number of ways.

History and Culture

Throughout the school year, the Center operates every weekday from 4:00 to 6:00 P.M. (thus offering not only its programs but also a safe place and a snack for children who have few other places to go). During the summer it meets every day for four weeks. Currently the program is held in a school, where it uses a number of rooms after classes and during vacation.

The breadth and depth of CCAL's offerings are unusual. The program is two-pronged. In the first track it offers a wide range of classes in the performing arts (instrumental and vocal music, dance) and the visual arts (drawing, painting, photography, ceramics, papermaking, etc.). A unique feature is that all of the children must participate in all of the arts; it's not a matter of choosing one or two.

There are several reasons behind this requirement. The staff argues that, most importantly, children respond differently to different opportunities and may need to experience several arts activities before they find what suits them. They also believe that all forms of the arts complement each other and that the experience of each is richer when they are juxtaposed.

At the same time, in the program's second track the children study the history of art from ancient Egypt to the 21st century. According to Heather McKay, the children benefit far more from their own arts activity if they know something about "where those arts came from and why." Teaching the arts of a particular period also includes learning about the culture from which that form developed.

In addition to their arts activities, the children work on reading and math skills and other subjects. There is always a relationship between those subjects and the art projects in process. For example, recently the children were studying dinosaurs in a Center science unit, so they made papier-mâché and clay

> The children benefit far more
> from their arts activity
> if they know something about
> "where those arts came from
> and why."

dinosaurs. They learn geometry in relation to forms in a painting or drawing. In spelling, the teachers turn the lessons into subjects for visual illustration.

The instructors also relate the various art forms to each other. For example, when learning about African or Latin American music, the children make and decorate their own drums or other instruments. In learning creative writing, they might write a story about dinosaurs, or space travel, or whatever else they are currently studying. At the end of each term, the children put on a festive performance and art show.

They sing, play musical instruments, perform dances, and read stories they have written. On tables and walls all around the room they display their drawings, paintings, ceramics, or other creations. Staff members encourage attendance by family and friends, as well as members of St. Andrew's and other congregations that have become involved in supporting the Center. The children's pride and excitement are visible as they sneak a look at someone special sitting in the audience. At a reception after the performance, everyone mingles and enjoys refreshments.

Developing Capacity

How did CCAL mushroom as it has? Connie Delzell is convinced that for every successful public ministry, there must be someone—lay or clergy—within the congregation "who's got the

---

You need that one person who is convinced that God wants this to be done

---

vision." In this case, of course, she was that person. She stresses the term *vision* rather than, say, *idea* to emphasize both a far-ranging imagination and a deep emotional and religious commitment to fulfilling the goal. "You need that one person," she continues, who "is convinced that God wants this to be done. If you start with a committee, it probably won't happen." Of course that inspired person can't function alone; the vision must become a shared one as it did at St. Andrew's.

Delzell is a staunch believer in congregations being practical and efficient in their business affairs. But she is also a risk taker. She and other early planners started by doing something symbolic of their determination to make the project work: painting and fixing up the church space where they hoped the program would take place. Then, she says, "we took a card table and sat under a tree in a housing project. Kids started coming over to see what we were doing." Even though careful planning must follow, there is also the necessity and the moment to jump into action and take that first risk. "You can kill a project by over-talking and over-planning," according to Delzell.

But quickly developing that organizational and administrative system is imperative. Delzell also realized early on the importance of creating a financial plan, not only for start-up but for perpetuation. She thinks a mistake earnest congregations often make is not being rigorous enough in financial planning, especially for the long range. St. Andrew's was a small congregation with few financial resources so Delzell went elsewhere for initial funding. She contacted some parishioners from her previous churches who she knew would be interested and had means. She also had a personal friend whom she convinced to provide start-up money of $10,000 over three years.

It's crucial to find that fine line between initial enthusiasm and having some basis to believe a project will work.

> A mistake earnest congregations often make is not being rigorous enough in financial planning, expecially for the long range.

Delzell thinks that "you need to be able to tolerate some chaos at first" and always be flexible, because no matter how carefully one plans, something will go wrong or change anyway.

Delzell felt it important to take some of that seed money to hire a secretary and a part-time grant writer. The first grant the Center received was from the city of Denver. Since the early years, others on staff have taken grant-writing classes and are very serious about learning this skill well. They subscribed to a magazine on grant writing and joined an organization of nonprofits that share information. As a result, they have achieved significant financial goals.

Nancee Martin-Coffey was the Center's development director in

2001-2002. In addition to preparing grant applications, the job includes making sure the CCAL receives publicity. The development director writes stories for local and religious publications and sends out press releases and photographs. The congregation produced a set of greeting cards featuring some of the children's artwork.

Volunteers and Professionals

At the same time the Center began raising money, it also set up training sessions for volunteers. These included understanding the situations the children came from, how to relate to and work with them, how to teach and tutor, and, of course, specifics about the classes' subject matter. Leaders developed a training booklet that they have continued to change as experience has warranted. There was constant support for volunteers, says Delzell: "We always had regular meetings to find out how volunteers were doing, what they needed, and so on."

At first, volunteers from St. Andrew's and Denver's Episcopal Cathedral conducted all Center programs. At the beginning, says Delzell, "We had 35 kids and 40 volunteers." But as the Center grew and expanded its hours, it became necessary to consider hiring professionals. Several other factors contributed to this decision, one that many programs started with volunteers must eventually face. For one thing, volunteers' schedules changed and the children had too little continuity in adult leadership. It became especially difficult to get volunteers who could work from 4:00 to 6:00 P.M., because of jobs or their own family commitments.

Both Delzell and Martin-Coffey stress the importance of matching volunteers with responsibilities that use their own gifts and skills. For instance, some of the artists in the parish might be hugely gifted but might have difficulty teaching, especially with children who

34

need extra structure and discipline. The CCAL participants enjoy the benefit of the professionals who bring with them a wide variety of experience.

There is still a need for volunteers, not only to help with the arts projects. They can also assist with organizational and administrative issues as well as tasks like providing transportation or snacks for the children. In fact, the volunteer pool has expanded well beyond the congregation. For example, it includes suburban congregations that supply resources, attend Center events, and at Christmas provide gifts for CCAL kids. In this way, the congregation's public has expanded not only in terms of those served but of those serving. For example, people from other denominations hear about CCAL, then call or show up to volunteer.

As the Center and its web of connections grow, how does Delzell—that original vision person—perpetuate the vision? She and the Center's other organizers work very hard at making sure the congregation stays actively involved. For example, a CCAL choir, the St. Cecelia singers, performs often at St. Andrew's. Some of the children's parents have become members of the church. Delzell and Martin-Coffey note that preaching includes frequent reference not just to the Center but to how it meshes with all the rest of the congregation's life.

Another ongoing Center–parish connection starts with Heather McKay. When she draws up plans for a new season of CCAL activities, she tries to elicit comments and ideas from congregation members. She is, she says, "always open to suggestions" from parishioners: "We have lots of professional artists in the parish who help us with ideas." Some members not only

---

Just as the presence of artists fostered what could be called an "attraction by similarity," the absence of children was an "attraction by difference."

35

contribute suggestions; they send their own children to the Center.

However, another reason the congregation feels so involved with CCAL is because, as one member commented, "We don't have many children in this congregation." That may change over time, but it was apparently a motivating factor in the church's original choice of ways to serve. Just as the presence of artists fostered what could be called an "attraction by similarity," the absence of children was an "attraction by difference." Both motivations are highly appropriate reasons for becoming involved in public ministry and strong incentives for continuing support.

Chapter 3

Learning by Example

Alfred Street Baptist Church
Alexandria, Virginia

On any given weekend Rosette Graham might make the 30-mile drive from her home to her church several times. Graham is a member of Alfred Street Baptist Church in Alexandria, Virginia, just outside Washington, D.C. This is a large African American congregation—some 2,000 members. Most are economically comfortable, though Graham remarks that some members receive food baskets whenever the congregation prepares them.

Graham is president of the church's Department of Missions (an elected position), so she may be at church more than some others. But many of Alfred Street's members spend an extraordinary amount of time there—certainly for worship services but also to participate in a huge variety of programs. They also spend a considerable amount of time away from the church but conducting the church's ministries.

Every aspect of church life includes a public component and a constant awareness that, in the words of the Reverend John O. Peterson, Sr., Alfred Street's pastor, "We offer ministry to all of mankind." Then he laughs: "Well, maybe not all . . ." Peterson also emphasizes that the church responds to the "physical and communal being" of people as well as to their spiritual needs. This emphasis is systemically incorporated into the congregation's public ministries in a variety of conscious and highly organized ways.

Alfred Street's directory lists 23 official ministries: everything from a health and wellness ministry to a sports/athletics ministry. There are drama and dance groups, as well as a huge music ministry comprising seven different choirs. Every one of these ministries is understood to have a role to play in the congregation's public outreach. And every member is expected to participate. It doesn't take long to become involved.

For example, Nadine Walker, a physician and recent church member, has already become very active in the congregation's growing AIDS ministry. When Dr. Walker came to Alfred Street, she immediately felt welcomed and encouraged to use her talents—not just her general medical skills but particular interests she has developed such as planning emotional support services to ac-company healing of the body. At Alfred Street there is a level of expectation that, because talents and skills are gifts from God, they are to be shared. Expressing a sentiment echoed by other members, Walker affirms that "God put me in this church."

Walker talks about her work

> Every one of these ministries is understood to have a role to play in the congregation's public outreach. And every member is expected to participate.

38

with the AIDS group. "We explain to different [church] departments how their focus can relate to AIDS," she says. This is true even of groups where the connection is not immediately obvious. "For example, we suggest what the drama ministry or the music ministry can do." Either of these might give a performance dramatizing the problems AIDS patients have. Walker believes that this crosscutting, interweaving attitude is basic to Alfred Street's success. "The approach is always more creative if we develop it as a [whole] congregation," she emphasizes.

Seeking Out the People

Part of Alfred Street's success is not just its variety of programs or their organizational structure, but the all-out way in which members seize, perform, and constantly seek to improve the ministries. For example, the church hosts a shelter for homeless people. But members also realize, in Rosette Graham's words, that "for a variety of reasons, many homeless people will not seek out a shelter. So Alfred Street seeks out the people." A regular program of the Department of Missions is to take food to wherever homeless people are located, especially in Washington, D.C., where the need is great. Volunteers prepare meals, usually for about 300, then pile into a couple of vans. Around eight people make the trip, which takes most of a day.

They set out for the areas of Washington where they know homeless people tend to gather. But they also just drive around looking for them, and they make as many unplanned stops as

Sometimes they lose their way in an unfamiliar part of the city, but that's all right too— it usually leads to the discovery of a new area of need.

39

planned ones. Sometimes they lose their way in an unfamiliar part of the city, but that's all right too—it usually leads to the discovery of a new area of need. They get out and carry food to people sitting on park benches, sleeping on the ground, or huddling along the side of a building seeking protection from the weather. They also take food to public shelters where the residents otherwise receive only one meal a day.

Washington is an important public for Alfred Street but the congregation also works with others. Though Alexandria itself is generally a prosperous community, there are pockets of want, according to Rosette Graham. The church's own neighborhood has an area of housing where, for example, drug dealers prey on residents. The church has been involved in building affordable housing and working with local police to improve the situation for current residents. Alfred Street also has a number of national and international ministries, focusing especially on the rural

south in the United States, where youth take yearly trips to do service projects, and on several countries in Africa.

Organizing a membership of 2,000 into structured teams to do ministry effectively can be complicated. It would be easy for a member to get lost in such a sizable population and to have a difficult time locating activities using his or her interests and skills. But there is a system for that—the same system that helps new members feel valued so quickly.

Whenever a new member joins, he or she immediately becomes part of a "Discipleship Group." These are clusters of around 30 members who are like a primary family within a larger extended family. They meet regularly for fellowship, as well as to choose and carry out programs that are part of the church's ministries. On a Saturday morning, a Discipleship Group might meet first for breakfast and then work on a project.

Assigned to each Discipleship Group is a trained deacon whose role is to lead and inspire—as much informally as formally. In addition to the deacon's receiving substantial training, his or her personality (usually outgoing and with a relaxed leadership style) will suit the position. Other deacons are leaders for the various ministries in which the Discipleship Group members can participate. The Board of Deacons (which currently has 42 members) meets regularly with the church's pastors. Among its responsibilities are to report on all of the groups' activities, to make church policy, and to act on new ideas from members.

A Special Focus on Youth

Beginning with young children, there is no age or activity at Alfred Street that does not incorporate a focus on public ministry. In the church's groups for "moms and babies" (three-year-olds), according to Reverend Peterson, "The first thing the children are taught is to get along with one another. There is no better forum than the church for learning to care for others."

Melanie Garrett, in her mid-20s, has grown up at Alfred Street. At every stage of her development, the church made her aware that "this church is an outreach church," she says. She recalls her first visit to a homeless shelter when she entered the junior youth group (ages 9 to 13). She also remembers playing with homeless children whom the youth group director brought home with her for brief stays.

According to Rosette Graham, for young people "church activities take precedence." When her daughter recently took a part-time job, she had to adjust the hours she worked to accommodate church participation. Another parent notes that his son had to coordinate basketball practice—and miss some games—because of the family's belief in making its faith commitments a priority.

Melanie Garrett thinks there are two

> **Young people see their parents and other adults engaged in public ministry, and they understand that it is an important part of their family's values as well as the church's.**

factors primarily responsible for the church's success in involving children and youth in public ministry. One is that all such activities are "made fun." There is always a great deal of "fellowship and community" so that, for example, young people don't feel they're making a big sacrifice if they spend their Saturdays painting homes for the elderly instead of meeting their friends at the mall. Laughter and singing—and eating—are important parts of any youth project.

Another point Garrett emphasizes is that "learning for children is done more by example than by instruction." Young people see their parents and other adults engaged in public ministry, and they understand that it is an important part of

their family's values as well as the church's. Parents at Alfred Street "are very involved with the youth ministries," says Garrett.

As the children become teenagers, the church pays a lot of attention to the challenges and problems that age group experiences. For instance, Alfred Street was one of the first churches in Virginia to conduct sexuality seminars for teens. The leaders took the teens' concerns seriously. In addition to their own leadership, they brought in a variety of youth ministers and theologians to discuss relevant issues. Because the young people have so many opportunities to express and process their own concerns, they develop a high degree of trust in adults and among themselves. They view the adults as mentors and tend to follow in their footsteps as they develop their own leadership skills. When they go out into the world, they are well prepared.

Melanie Garrett thinks that Alfred Street's overall emphasis on doing things in groups, as well as *how* that's done, is important, "especially for a young person, when you are looking for approval. Kids become more confident and creative." When Garrett went to college in Indiana, the unusual amount of experience she'd had at Alfred Street put her in a position to lead the college's Christian youth group.

Beginning a New Ministry

Another key to Alfred Street's success in public ministry is the considerable care it takes in deciding whether to start a new ministry. Once a decision has been made to go forward, the same care then distinguishes its development. A recent example is the congregation's decision to begin a ministry for deaf people.

Congregation member Karen DeSandies has a brother who is hearing-impaired. She was a speech pathology major in college, and has always been interested in the relationship of hearing and language. In May of 2000 she drew up a proposal for Alfred Street to begin a ministry with deaf people. When she first began talking about it, she says, "People would say, 'We don't need such a ministry here. We don't have any deaf members.'" That's exactly the point, according to DeSandies. Her standard reply was, "They don't come here because we don't have anything for them." Her arguments sparked the congregation's awareness and interest.

DeSandies did considerable research and marshaled her facts. For example, she could tell parishioners that there are 12,500 deaf individuals in northern Virginia, but that most churches' services are "geared for hearing." She also demonstrated that deaf people fall through the cracks in receiving all kinds of social services

---

Young people view the adults as mentors and tend to follow in their footsteps as they develop their own leadership skills.

43

because "they're not mainstreamed" and not organized to press for their rights.

She also suggested how all the various groups within the church could incorporate services for deaf people into their ministries. She invited experts to give seminars on setting up a ministry for deaf people. She began learning sign language and later took intensive training at the Iowa School for the Deaf.

These are the sorts of steps congregants pursue when they have an idea for a new ministry. As a result of DeSandies' efforts and the congregation's decision to support the ministry, sign interpretation of Sunday services began in January 2002. DeSandies has a list of additional projects she would like to introduce, such as a ministry to deaf people with AIDS, and setting up a center for reading to deaf children. But before she proceeds, the congregation will see how the program's early stages work out, and will then apply the same sorts of careful questions about need and resources to any new phases.

Another member of the congregation is currently pursuing the idea of a ministry with single parents. She is in the first stages of exploring need and capacity, and will go through the same kinds of steps described above. According to Reverend Peterson, he asked her to "think through the mission [and] see if it fills a gap" as well as to consider whether Alfred Street would be a logical host. When she has compiled preliminary information, she will present it to the ministerial staff, who have a process for considering it. If they are enthused, the word will go out to others. Eventually, if all the questions seem to have positive answers, the idea will go to the Board of Deacons.

Pulling It All Together

There is no doubt that part of Alfred Street's success in developing ministries is its size. But the basic principles according to which the congregation operates have little to do with size alone: the emphasis on valuing every member's skills and putting them to work; the availability of ministries to suit different interests; breaking down the membership into smaller groups to make people feel welcome and intimately connected. Also crucial are the special focus on youth and the presence of designated procedures for introducing and exploring new ideas. All of these elements, according to Peterson, are tied closely to a strong biblical base that he and his colleagues consistently emphasize in worship.

A dramatic symbol of how the congregation regards all of its ministries is its elaborate yearly Christmas pageant. There is something for everyone to do. If you're not on stage acting or singing or dancing or speaking, you're operating lights or sound equipment or some other essential activity.

So many members of so many ages participate, it seems like there would be no one in the audience. But there is:

the public. The congregation considers its performances public events, and invites the whole community. In addition to friends and neighbors, visitors include residents of a nearby nursing home who arrive in buses.

Performers are exhausted after the three-hour pageant, but there's no decrease in attendance at the regular Sunday worship service the next morning. And then the members all reassemble again Sunday night for another pageant performance. Monday night they will be back at the church for meetings and projects to support their other ongoing public ministries.

CHAPTER 4

"HEALING THE WORLD"

KEHILLAT ISRAEL SYNAGOGUE
PACIFIC PALISADES, CALIFORNIA

K ehillat Israel is a Reconstructionist Jewish synagogue in Pacific Palisades, California. Though officially a part of Los Angeles, the mostly upscale enclave on the far western edge of the city acts in many ways like a suburb. It would be easy to ignore the tangle of needs and wants in the inner city. But the temple's location is a metaphor for the engagement it has chosen to have with the metropolis. The famed Sunset Boulevard, which runs all through Los Angeles—including some of its poorest and its richest neighborhoods—continues right to the corner where the synagogue is situated.

Reconstructionism, which originated in the United States in the 1920s, is the youngest among the four branches of American Judaism (the other groups are Orthodox, Conservative, and Reform). It seeks to combine traditional spiritual values with an

> Reconstructionism recognizes that every people and every culture has its own unique and valuable contribution to make to the progress of humanity.

emphasis on the immediate circumstances in which contemporary congregations find themselves. Public outreach is a key component of Reconstructionist belief. Kehillat Israel literature states that Reconstructionism "recognizes that every people and every culture has its own unique and valuable contribution to make to the progress of humanity."

Rabbi Steven Carr Reuben came to Kehillat Israel in 1986, called by the congregation specifically because of his reputation for outreach leadership. (In previous congregations he had done especially innovative work with homeless people.) Reuben believes the key to faithful living is for a congregation to demonstrate its values in public and physical form: to "walk the talk," he says.

Membership at Kehillat Israel is currently around 2,500 (900+ households). It wasn't always so large: it has grown ever since Reuben arrived and has doubled in the past six years. Most members ascribe the growth to the public service for which the temple has become well known since the rabbi's arrival.

Reuben sums up his theology this way: humans are "co-partners with God in completing the work of creation. We are God's hands, eyes, and mouth." Kehillat Israel is known not only for the number and variety of its outreach programs, but also for the particular way in which congregation members become involved. Every year during the High Holy Days, which include the Jewish New Year, it is regular practice at synagogues to make a financial appeal for the following year. Members are encouraged to make a special donation. Reuben believes that the practice of focusing on money runs the risk of "diminishing the sanctity of the message." He uses that time, instead, to preach on and to make an appeal for a commitment to outreach.

Members fill out a special Tikun Olam ("healing the world") pledge card, which lists the ten or so official task forces the synagogue has chosen for particular focus. Reuben stresses the importance of avoiding "fill in the blank" answers or general references to the projects in favor of "specific descriptive choices." Members commit to serving on one or more of the task forces during the next year (such a commitment is invited but not required). A special ceremony includes bringing the cards forward and dedicating them.

There are other similar occasions such as "Mega Mitzvah Day" (mitzvah = a good deed), when members pledge to make outreach commitments. During its 50th anniversary year in 2001, the congregation collectively pledged to contribute "one million mitzvah minutes" to public service.

Specific Mitzvah Opportunities

When Reuben came to Kehillat Israel, he knew this was a congregation where people had great interest but relatively little experience in public service. The temple, he says, had a social action committee "which consisted of 20 people in a room arguing. Little things got done but nothing on the scale of what I knew this congregation could do." He reasoned that "if 20 people with three interests create three groups, it's better than taking the lowest common denominator for all 20."

He saw his first task as, simply, to "talk to people"—many people, not just those on the social action committee—to learn about their interests or what might fire their imaginations. Reuben refers to "very specific mitzvah opportunities"—specific to the individual. When he made his first effort with a High Holy Days sermon on outreach, accompanied by distribution

> **For any potential task force to be adopted, at least one congregation member must already be involved in it.**

of service pledge cards, the result was immediate enthusiasm and vigorous participation, he says.

The initial group of projects from which members could select was based on their own interests as the rabbi had heard them described. He helped the new task forces set up their first meetings and then "left them to decide their agenda. Immediately, lay people took over." After that, "I came to meetings only when they wanted me to," he explains. Both the pledge process and the shape of the overall social action program have gone through various changes. Now they run "pretty much on their own," says Reuben.

Members often suggest new task forces to begin or to "adopt." Adopting means choosing to provide official Kehillat Israel support to a project already in existence. In either case, the idea person must draw up a detailed organizational plan that includes specifics, such as how they propose to raise money for the project, how many people would be required, what kind of space, what sorts of materials, and so on.

Along the way, they check in with the congregation's executive director, who is in charge of all business matters. The director is prepared to advise them on a variety of issues, including finances. Occasionally that must include saying no. The director must sometimes tell a member that the temple does not have the budget or capacity for a particular project, or that for some other reason it would not be advisable going further with an idea. But if there is no cause for discouragement, there is then a specific procedure for the board to consider a new task force.

For any potential task force to be adopted, at least one congregation member must already be involved in it.

50

In other words, members can't just hear about a worthy program and suggest that the congregation support it. The proposer must already be active and have ideas about how to draw in other members of the congregation. When a new program begins, there is training for task force leaders. A big part of that training is in "the care and feeding of volunteers," with an emphasis on strong and continuing support for them. Leaders write detailed descriptions of responsibilities, call with frequent reminders, and express regular thanks for members' involvement.

Using Individual Skills

The temple lists ten or so official task forces—some begun by members, others the congregation has adopted. An example of the first category is the Extra Helpings Westside Task Force generated and organized by congregation member Bruce Rosen. Rosen is an investment advisor who has become a mainstay of the congregation's Tikun Olam program. He was concerned about combating hunger in the Los Angeles area's many poor sections. At first, as he describes it, "I did the standard food pantry stuff," passing out canned goods and other nonperishable items to needy people.

As important as this was, Rosen began to feel that this "wasn't the best use of my skills"—the managerial and administrative capabilities he had developed over the years. He was frustrated with the program's lack of order. "The pantry would sometimes run out of food before the end of the day," he says. He decided he might better use his skills and talents to take on organizational responsibilities—for example, doing adequate advance planning to ensure a constant supply of food.

Rosen is definitely not shy. He began visiting local grocery stores to ask for donations of food. He was surprised at the overwhelmingly positive response; they simply hadn't been asked before.

He started out, he says, "with a car and a dolly." Every day he drove his car around to the stores and delivered their contributions to the pantry. He planned and budgeted both time and resources to fit the needs. Soon he realized the necessity for a larger and more comprehensive operation. The result was Extra Helpings Westside, which became one of the temple's official projects.

Other members began picking up and delivering the food. This was especially appealing, for example, to retired people who had the time and the cars to do the driving. The project was so successful that Rosen had to establish a nonprofit corporation to support its work. By the late 1990s, the agency was covering the whole west side of Los Angeles and distributing over 100,000 pounds of food per month. Its goal, according to Rosen, was "that there should be no food wasted in a community where people have to struggle to feed themselves."

Up and Out

One of the congregation's adopted Tikun Olam projects is Chrysalis, a nonprofit agency that helps unemployed poor and homeless people find jobs. Chrysalis President Adlai Wertman and Community Outreach Director Fran Leb are both members of Kehillat Israel and brought it into the congregation's family of task forces. Now other temple members volunteer to help with various activities.

These are almost limitless since Chrysalis helps clients with every aspect of preparing for and holding a job. They include a wide range of classes such as computer training, resumé writing, and interview skills. The agency provides

---

There should be no food wasted in a community where people have to struggle to feed themselves.

---

clothing for interviews. It offers office tools such as phones, copying, and fax machines. Once people have a job, Chrysalis provides job retention services that include workshops and individual counseling. It also runs its own business called "StreetWorks," a street-cleaning operation that has contracts with business associations and government departments. It teaches cleaning skills and provides employment, having become so busy that it operates 24 hours a day, seven days a week.

Another of the synagogue's adopted task forces serves a dramatically different public: children living in war-torn areas around the world. Established by Judith Jenya, who later joined Kehillat Israel, the Global Children's Organization (GCO) has organized summer camps in disturbed areas such as Bosnia or Northern Ireland. The camps bring together children from opposing sides of a conflict. They have an opportunity for respite and a chance to realize what it's like to live without the constant presence of violence. In addition to experiencing fun and recreation, the campers learn nonviolent ways of resolving differences.

Jenya notes that "the parents also benefit." In Northern Ireland, for example, limited finances forced Catholic and Protestant parents to cooperate in hiring a bus to transport the children to camp. That cooperation may not have led to a comprehensive dialogue, but it was a step in the right direction.

Kehillat Israel members, especially children and young people, help GCO by collecting the many types of supplies the camps need. Other volunteers help Jenya with a distribution system to ship the supplies to their destinations. Some members have paid their own way to work at the summer camps.

On Their Own Terms

The congregation itself has a strong focus on children and young people. Its Early Childhood Center serves parents and their children as young as two-and-a-half. There is also a Family Religious School that covers the years from kindergarten to confirmation. Prominent among its programs is an emphasis on what Temple literature describes as "our core Jewish spiritual value of 'Tikun Olam,' Jewish ethics for 'repairing the world.'" In the religious school all children must develop their own "mitzvah project." It could be linked to a task force or be a one-time event of the child's choosing and planning.

Other youth activities include a Junior Congregation that meets monthly, confirmation preparation programs for grades 8–12 that "engage young people in a wide variety of ethical action projects and social issues," and a youth lounge where young members and their friends

---

Kid's don't realize they have power. They feel powerless. We emphasize that each one can do something to change another life.

---

of all faiths can either drop by or engage in organized activities and projects.

Bruce Rosen of Extra Helpings Westside describes how these principles carry over to daily living in the congregation's families. It's important, he says, for children to learn about social problems in their own terms. For instance, he notes, "Most hunger programs are impersonal. You donate or bring cans. You don't get any connection. This doesn't help kids understand." So with his own children (ages 12, 9, and 4), he has them plan and prepare (to the extent they can) a meal for a child. "Sometimes they put in a gift," he says. The children personally deliver the meal.

This "child-to-child" emphasis is present throughout the congregation's programs. "Kids don't realize they have power," says Rosen. "They feel powerless. We emphasize that each one can do something to change another life. This is constantly being talked about by the clergy. It makes the message of their sermons."

Rabbi Reuben believes that a key element in the success of Kehillat Israel's outreach programs is their relationship to worship and spirituality. The congregation's worship is a blend of traditional and newer practices. For example, Reuben is as apt to pick up his guitar and sing to make a point as he is to deliver it in prose. The musical treatment might be contemporary but the words of the message can come from age-old traditions.

The congregation does not regard service as something separate from worship; it is an essential part of it. Sermons, prayers, and music often relate to particular types of outreach as well as to religious holidays or other important events. For a recent Sabbath service on Labor Day weekend, for example, Reuben preached about the meaning and sanctity of work and its importance for developing human dignity.

There were also guest speakers. Vivian Rothstein, coordinator of an organization called the Living Wage Initiative, talked about how these principles of human dignity are sacred to Judaism and how important it is to extend them to other groups. She brought with her two Latina women who work as hotel maids and who are struggling to earn decent wages and obtain better treatment from their employers.

An emphasis on spirituality also characterizes the temple's education programs. For example, Associate Rabbi Sheryl Lewart teaches a variety of classes and workshops on Jewish spirituality. She relates spirituality to how congregants can "target our gifts and services to the broad scope of populations" whom they encounter. She also does individual spiritual direction with members.

A Community without Walls

Most of the Tikun Olam task forces serve persons of every religion or none. But some are designed for particular Jewish publics. One is the Russian

Connection Task Force that assists the large number of Russian Jewish immigrants living in the Los Angeles area. In addition to teaching language skills, the program provides training in Jewish theology and practice for people who grew up without that preparation. Kehillat Israel members invite these immigrants to temple services and to their homes, as well as accompanying them to cultural events.

Lewart also describes another group the temple's education programs serve: American Jews who have little training in traditional practices. Classes include Hebrew literacy, how to study religious texts, "Jewish Life in America," and how to maintain a Jewish home observing traditional customs. These programs attract participants from all over the Los Angeles area. They take place at different times of day and evening to accommodate people's schedules. For those who can't otherwise get to the temple, congregation members pick them up.

Lewart notes that the education program will soon incorporate the technology for a distance-learning component. Allowing people to register for courses electronically, she says, will further develop her concept of "a community without walls." "Our education public ministry connects people not only with each other, but with the larger Jewish community everywhere. This is a very real public. We meet them through learning," she says.

Kehillat Israel is a congregation that could easily decide to contribute a lot of money to worthwhile projects and let it go at that. In deciding just the opposite, it's clear that "healing the world" means to members that they must go physically into that world. They are compelled to move beyond the impersonal act of writing a check, as worthwhile as that can be, to share their skills and talents as well as their incomes; to involve themselves directly and personally in work that is part of their religious mandate.

CHAPTER 5

A COMMITMENT TO HOPE

DUGAN ALTERNATIVE HIGH SCHOOL
HOLY CROSS/IMMACULATE HEART OF MARY ROMAN CATHOLIC CHURCH,
CHICAGO, ILLINOIS

C hicago winters are long and harsh. Residents anxiously
await the first warm spring day when they can go outdoors
and rejoice in the change. But not everyone rejoices, and
not everyone rushes outside. Many children and teenagers in the
southside neighborhood called Back of the Yards stay in. That's
because the gangs are out, celebrating their own release from winter
confinement. They celebrate by driving their cars up and down the
streets, firing their guns. It's too easy for someone on the sidewalk
or sitting on the front stoop to be in the way of a stray bullet.

This area is home to Holy Cross/Immaculate Heart of Mary
Roman Catholic Church (HCIHM), which has developed a unique
ministry to serve city teenagers and to make the neighborhood
safer: an alternative high school that accepts drop-outs or youth
who have been expelled from other schools. Its success has

changed not only the school's students, but the parish and the community as well.

The "Yards" takes its name from its years as location of the city's bustling stockyards, though that industry is now essentially gone. As it waned, the neighborhood, down on its luck and down in the heels, became home to many Mexican immigrants—some legal, some not—seeking better economic prospects in a new country.

Now the area is almost entirely Mexican: primarily the working poor struggling to earn enough to make ends meet. These mostly recent residents work so hard, in fact, that they may hold two or three jobs and be at home only long enough to grab a few hours of sleep between shifts. One HCIHM member tells a story that she "woke up one day and forgot where to go."

The hard work and dedication of these determined newcomers, many of them HCIHM parishioners, has had a bitterly ironic result. Because their children are so often left alone, they grow up without much supervision or guidance. They spend their time on the streets with nowhere particular to go and no healthy goals to pursue. By the time they reach their teens, they are likely to become a statistic in the neighborhood's staggering 70 percent high school dropout rate.

Cruel Temptations

Some youth leave school because they succumb to the pressure or lure of joining a gang. The gangs offer a feeling of belonging, a sense of identity, and a set of rules for living that the teens were not otherwise receiving. They can also offer an income—usually through selling drugs—to kids who have none. Other students drop out because they fear the power and violence of the gangs in the school hallways as well as on the streets.

In February 1998 the violence in the area reached a peak when two youth, ages 12 and 13, shot and killed a younger boy. While HCIHM had sponsored social programs combating violence and gang influence, the murder was a catalyst that propelled the church into an entirely new public ministry. The Reverend Bruce Wellems, C.M.F., HCIHM's pastor (known as Father Bruce), vowed "that the church would find new ways to break the cycle of gangs and violence." He saw that what the youth needed was "attention, education, and stability in a safe and welcoming environment."

Working with staff colleagues and church members, Wellems helped HCIHM establish Dugan Alternative High School to serve as such a place. Its namesake is the late Sister Irene Dugan, R.C., his spiritual director. Dugan opened its doors in the fall of 1998, less than a year after the shooting that had prompted it. The parish is at the heart of th eprogram, which is funded by the Chicago Public School System. Since it opened, Dugan has been so successful at keeping

> **Father Bruce vowed that the church would find new ways to break the cycle of gangs and violence.**

teens in school until graduation that it has inspired another church-sponsored alternative school nearby.

One reason establishing the school took relatively little time was that HCIHM already had a history of public outreach during Wellems's tenure. When he came to the church in 1990, he says, "I asked the congregation to tell me my mission"—based, of course, on the congregation's mission. "Was I to raise money? Was I to serve the poor? Which poor? How do we define poor?" The congregation presented Wellems with a mission of several parts, an important one of which was "to serve youth at risk" since that group was such a vulnerable part of the parish's public. Drawing from that discussion of mission, Wellems helped the congregation further develop its capacity for public ministry.

59

An important early stage of that development process was the congregation's probe of its feelings about public education. According to Wellems, some parish members thought that in addressing teens' problems it would be a good idea for the church to establish a parochial school and to control its quality and subject matter. Wellems asked them to reconsider. "The answer is not just to build a Catholic school," he argued, "but to support and help reform the public school system."

His recommendation was not only for the benefit of the students, but of parishioners themselves. "In order to have power and influence, you must figure out the system on your own; you must know how the system works," he explained. This was an especially important message for recent immigrants who basically felt overwhelmed by "the system"—whether the education system, city government, or any other bureaucracy. This was a convincing argument, and when Wellems later proposed the alternative high school, the idea did not fall on deaf ears.

Certainly another reason the process of developing Dugan went so quickly is because of Father Bruce's outgoing personality and his determination. For example, shortly after he submitted an application to the city for a start-up grant, he showed up at the Chicago Public Schools office to check on its status. He wasn't going to leave without an answer. He discovered that "the application was sitting in a big pile of others," and his visit helped to speed up the evaluation process.

Limits and Standards

Dugan can enroll a maximum of 30 students at a time (it has plans to expand), and there is always a waiting list. Its current enrollment is about 80 percent youth from the immediate neighborhood, 20 percent from further away. A few are children of parishioners. But the staff of the church and the school understands the concept of a parish broadly. There are no geographical restrictions within the city for students to apply to Dugan. According to Sister Angie Kolacinski, S.H., a parish pastoral associate, "We don't consider our parish to be just those who come to church here." Teens or their parents hear about the school through various means: the police, probation officers, social workers, or word of mouth.

The school operates in two small rooms in a church building that also has a tiny computer lab and a single office shared by the three full-time and several part-time teachers. Students can stay in the school pursuing graduation until they are 21. They study the standard subjects required for a high school diploma such as math, U.S. history, and social studies. (Since Dugan is a publicly funded school there is, of course, no religious instruction.)

According to head teacher Brigitte Swenson, the staff works hard to "adapt the materials to students' experiences and to develop teaching methods appropriate to their skills and ways of learning." This includes a great deal of personal attention. The three full-timers meet with each other every day to compare notes and constantly revise and refine how they teach. "We'll do whatever it takes" to make sure the kids learn, says Swenson. But that does not include relaxing standards. "Often, kids who come here are motivated to finish high school, but that doesn't mean they're necessarily motivated to work hard," she explains. Part of the teachers' responsibility is to instill that motivation.

On the other hand, Dugan staff members are sensitive to their students' additional needs, which often include the absolute necessity of holding a job to earn some money for their family.

Father Bruce's two tenets: "It's never too late to change, and "youth must have a commitment to hope."

"We respect their boundaries," she says, and the staff works flexibly to demonstrate support. They all subscribe to Father Bruce's two basic tenets: One is that "it's never too late for change," and the other is his insistence that the youth must have "a commitment to hope."

Recruiting Mentors

Dugan receives help in various forms from diverse individuals and groups in the Chicago area. For example, according to HCHIM's employment and training coordinator, Marco Lopez, who works with the Dugan students, it has a number of partnerships with businesses in its immediate community and beyond. Some of these have sponsored scholarships or contributed supplies such as books. Others work with staff to help students find jobs, both while they are in school and after they graduate.

Some of these businesses are struggling themselves, yet, according to Lopez, "People in the business community are willing to mentor," even if they are having their own problems. Students might start with office or factory work, truck deliveries, store cashiering, or hotel employment. Some have gone on to jobs as bank tellers and construction managers. Several have enrolled in college.

Lopez also works with the students "to help them get ready for the job market," teaching them how to fill out an application, for instance. He might ask a banker to visit to explain how to write a check and hold a bank account. "These kids need life skills," Lopez says; "they need to learn how to manage time and how to deal with anger and frustration in healthy ways." The jobs programs have benefits beyond the employee, says Lopez. "Whenever a young person gets a job, the word spreads" and helps to foster a sense of hope and energy. Dugan students are also required to participate in community activities. Choices include park clean-up, working with young children in an after-school program, and feeding the homeless. Or the youth can come up with their own project.

School and Congregation

All of these factors—small classes, individual attention, flexible teaching, cooperation with area businesses and organizations, having the students participate in community activities— have contributed to Dugan's success. But, according to Father Bruce, the real key is that "the church is at the heart of the program." What he's referring to is the remarkable participation by parishioners even though they may not have children at the school and it is not a religious institution.

The plan to establish the school was not without criticism, even though the stage had been set earlier with the resolution of the public/parochial school discussion. Some parishioners worried that having a group including former

There is remarkable participation by parishioners even though they may not have children at school and it is not a religious institution.

gang members meeting every day on church grounds would create a threat to their own children, including those who attend a grade school across the street.

The staff took several immediate steps to inform and reassure these parents. There were meetings held to discuss the idea. When members raised fears, they were taken seriously. According to HCHIM youth worker Oscar Contreras, a step-by-step approach worked best. For example, he asked the parishioners whether "you actually know any of these kids?" Then the group discussed the process of how stereotypes develop and why it's important not to base decisions on them. They convened dinners at which the teens and the parishioners could meet.

63

The end result was full support from the parish. In fact, says Norene Baltazar, Dugan school secretary and parish member, adults at HCIHM have come to "adopt" the teenagers, especially those who travel from other parts of the city. They continue to hold get-acquainted dinners, for which the students have written many letters of thanks. They host receptions and provide refreshments. Church volunteers help with school events and in arranging ceremonies like graduation, which they always attend.

Parishioners conduct fundraising projects, and they have presented the students with Christmas gifts. "For many of the kids," says Father Bruce, "this is the first time they've received a gift." Sometimes Dugan students participate in trips organized for parish youth. An example might be a bus ride to an entertainment area, the zoo, or a park. Many of the young people have never before visited downtown Chicago.

Another important way in which the congregation has embraced the school is through a series of programs designed not for the kids but for parents. These programs address root problems that can spawn trouble for children. For example, HCIHM member Miroslava Vasquez, a social worker, directs a series of parenting classes offered through the church. So far, she says, some 500 parents have been through the program. Parishioners came to realize that even if their children aren't in the school or involved in gangs, they can still benefit from the parenting groups.

"The parents themselves need help in dealing with their own problems," says Vasquez, "which can include alcoholism or drug use, domestic violence, and lack of self-esteem." There are ample reasons for the parents' difficulties. According to Vasquez, many "may have gone only through second or third grade themselves. And it is not uncommon where they came from [mostly rural Mexico] to get married at 15, even younger." Says Vasquez, the parenting program is "the right hand to the outreach."

The workshops tackle such issues as how to nurture a healthy marriage; how to communicate within a family; how to practice discipline without corporal punishment; and why an education is important. In addition, parents learn how crucial it is for them to play a strong role in their children's lives.

Walking the Aisles

The worship at HCIHM relates to the high school program in a variety of ways. First, there is a major emphasis on young people. On a typical Sunday, children and teens (some of them Dugan students) play a variety of important parts in the Mass. One of the most prominent is their role as primary suppliers of the service's music. Wellems started a program teaching kids how to play marimbas, mariachis, and other instruments popular in Mexican culture. They also sing. The music is almost all Mexican, and all Mass participants participate loudly. Young parents or grandparents sway babies rhythmically to the beat.

In addition to providing music for worship, the teens give a recital every six weeks. They also play for events all around the city, such as weddings or other celebrations, picnics, or civic events. Proceeds from their performances—some $25,000 annually—have paid for the parish's parenting program.

Wellems preaches in a way especially appealing to young people. He never stays still for long, moving up and down the aisles. He often speaks directly to them, sometimes by individual name. He uses examples that relate directly to their lives. He'll occasionally break out of Spanish into English slang that all the young people understand—suggesting that he is indeed delivering a special message to them.

This lively worship is actually very appealing to all ages in the congregation, who pack the church for a weekend's eight Masses. People come whenever their work schedules allow, more than once if possible. Total attendance for the weekend can be anywhere from 3,000 to 5,000, according to Wellems.

After morning Mass, there is a substantial meal for all who want to attend. Families tend to linger long after the service is over. The extended time provides one of the neighborhood's basic social opportunities for both adults and children. All ages mix, and older children watch over younger ones. Teens might sit with their parents or their friends. At one of these events, one teenage parishioner who is also a Dugan student was heard making audible groans. She's anxious to be off with her friends, remarking that she "gets too much attention here." Everywhere she goes around the church or school, she says, "I've got seven adults on my back." But she says this only half ruefully.

CHAPTER 6

PUBLIC HEALTH AND THE PRIVATE SOUL

SHEPHERD'S HAND CLINIC,
CHRIST LUTHERAN CHURCH
WHITEFISH, MONTANA

Speaking before a group has never been Meg Erickson's favorite activity. As a skilled and dedicated nurse, she would much rather spend her time in the practice of her profession. But there she is on a Sunday morning, speaking from the pulpit of Christ Lutheran Church to the 400 or so parishioners packing the sanctuary. Erickson will do almost anything if it's in the service of Shepherd's Hand Clinic, the free medical ministry she administers in the church building with her physician husband, Jay Erickson, and a host of other volunteers. The Ericksons are members of the congregation in the small town of Whitefish, Montana, where the clinic has been operating successfully since late 1995, filling a significant need. Every so often Meg Erickson brings the congregation up to date on the clinic's latest developments.

Whitefish is located in the state's remote northwestern corner, not far from Glacier National Park. The town's economy depends largely on tourism. Here in the mountains, the tourist season is confined primarily to the warm months. Even with an increase in winter sports, jobs in the tourism industry still tend to be seasonal and temporary. Most carry no benefits. That means, above all, no health insurance.

Businesses directly or indirectly serving tourism include motels, restaurants, nightspots, recreational facilities, clothing or sporting goods stores, and gift shops. In fact, almost everyone in town depends at least partially on tourism for economic support. The area's employers are not a bunch of hard-hearted, penny-pinching grinches. Many of them would like to be able to provide employee health insurance but work under the same economic and seasonal restrictions as their workers do, and are simply not able to afford it.

The tourism workers are often young adults drawn to the area for its natural beauty and the idea of living "close to nature." They frequently come to Whitefish without a job, optimistic and full of expectation. Other tourism employees are longtime residents whose education or other circumstances have limited their job opportunities to waitressing, cleaning cabins, kitchen work, or grounds up-keep.

The Ericksons came to Whitefish in the early 1990s from the Midwest. The longer they practiced medicine in the new location, the more they noticed increases in the number of people unable to afford even basic medical care. Having chosen their vocations in the first place as a way living out their faith, the Ericksons found the situation distressing. They discussed the problem with other parishioners, and at a church council retreat in early 1995, says Meg Erickson, "The idea for a free clinic, as a mission outreach, was born." After careful research and preparation, the

68

clinic opened in October of that year.

Since that time, the clinic has served between 800 and 1,200 patients per year and, at one time, had to turn away some. It simply could not accommodate all the people from the wider geographical area who showed up needing care. Fortunately, the demonstration of need and Shepherd Hand's success inspired a second clinic in nearby Kalispell, run by the Salvation Army.

Shepherd's Hand is completely lay organized and lay led, but the pastors are "very supportive," according to Meg Erickson, and the ministry operates in the context of the congregation's overall theology and mission. According to the Reverend John Bent, senior pastor at Christ Lutheran, it reflects a conscious process the congregation undertook to "move from a control-based ministry to a mission-based ministry. We needed to take our eyes off of ourselves," he explains. The first step in this process, says Bent, was "worship-renewal . That had to come before anything else."

The reason we exist as a church is for the sake of those who aren't here.

According to Bent, part of rethinking worship led to this conclusion: "The reason we exist as a church is for the sake of those who aren't here"—that is, those who are outside the church. The clinic is "an expression of our faith," says Bent. It has "opened the congregation's eyes" and helped members see that ministry belongs to the whole people of God. It has even changed some views about the church building itself. Some used to worry that "if other people come in, they might mess it up." Now, Bent comments, "nearly everyone is interested in the many ways can we use our building for our community?"

A Quick Transformation

Shepherd's Hand Clinic meets once a week in the evening. The work starts with volunteers delving into church closets to take out the stored medical equipment and supplies. They quickly transform church rooms into various kinds of medical facilities. The social room becomes an intake and waiting area where the workers set up tables and chairs. Magazines are available for patients to pass the time, as are toys for children. Sometimes the church's youth group or other volunteers supply cookies.

The two pastors' offices become medical examining rooms, their regular furniture temporarily moved aside to accommodate wheeled examining tables. Another area becomes a makeshift pharmacy, where volunteer Bob Grady, a retired pharmacist, holds careful discussions with patients and either dispenses prescribed medications donated by local pharmacies or gives the patient a voucher that a pharmacy will fill.

Another source of medicine is physician-donated samples. Grady was the clinic's first volunteer, and has not missed a night since its opening.

The entire clinic staff are volunteers, with Meg Erickson functioning as clinic administrator. All work on a rotating basis, serving as often as they can. In addition to church members, there are volunteers from other churches, civic organizations, and the entire community. There is currently a waiting list of volunteers. The Ericksons have recruited doctors, nurses, and other medical professionals from local practices and hospitals. Usually there are two physicians and a nurse on duty whenever the clinic is open. Hospitals and specialists take referrals for clinic patients who have serious problems such as a major illness or a need for surgery. In such cases, there are ways to help a patient finance very large expenditures.

Carefully trained volunteers fill out detailed questionnaires with each patient about his or her health and financial circumstances. An evening's problems will range from flu symptoms, to follow-up on chronic heart conditions or diabetes, to job injuries. The latter are common among the area's self-employed construction workers who might be helping to build a new motel or a house for a wealthy summer vacationer. One night, a Ukranian immigrant who couldn't speak English arrived in a van driven by his son. He was experiencing back pain so severe that he couldn't walk, so the doctor went out to see him in the parking lot.

The staff always tries to see children first. The volunteers, including the physicians, dress in jeans or other casual wear to put patients at ease. Communication is informal—and strictly confidential. In a small town, patients are sensitive about receiving medical "charity" and don't want it voiced about. Volunteers are careful to oblige. For example, Rich Dolven, a local school principal and member of Christ Church works as a behind-the-scenes office

> The clinic has "given a direction" to generalized wishes to help and has concretized the church's mission.

helper processing paper instead of doing something more visible like intake. He doesn't want to embarrass parents or children whom he may see the next day at school. Dolven notes that the clinic has had an interesting effect on the congregation and on his own spiritual life. It has "given a direction" to generalized wishes to help and has concretized the church's mission.

"It's the Economy"

Many of the clinic patients are working people and reluctant to seek charity. According to Meg Erickson, "68 percent of our patients make less than $11,000 per year even though 50 percent of them are employed." For those who are unemployed for health reasons, one of the clinic's goals is to help them become well enough to hold a job. Even then, though, the insurance problem may remain.

Just as all work is performed by volunteers, all finances and supplies are donated—by individuals and groups from the church and the larger community. Some of the financial contributors include small businesses that would like to provide health insurance for their employees but can't afford it.

For example, two members of Christ Church own a local pub and music spot. Their employees do not receive benefits. The pub owners make financial contributions to the clinic as well as volunteering when it is in session. Other community donations have included low-cost bank loans for patients with major medical expenses.

Patients frequently offer to make various types of contributions in kind. One volunteered to mow the church's grass and shovel snow. When patients have died, family members have donated their unopened medications back to the clinic to help others.

Clinic development was deliberate and methodical. The first step was to establish a steering committee whose initial responsibility was to identify and probe need. That group conducted local research, contacting the county health department, local hospitals, and physicians. Two goals were to avoid duplication of services and to build a sense of community interest and support. For example, the county has an immunization program so the clinic did not include that in its plans. A key to success at every stage, says Erickson, was "a lot of communication."

Steering committee members also researched how other free clinics around the country (not necessarily church-related) have managed and what lessons they have learned. They came at the issue from another side, too: How had other churches dealt with health-care needs in their own location?

Step two, networking within the

community, included purchasing a mailing list from the local Chamber of Commerce and contacting all of its members for their advice and support. They also met one-on-one with local bankers and with community leaders to introduce the idea of the clinic and request feedback. The goal was to build community awareness, interest, and potential for cooperation. The organizers wanted to emphasize that this new ministry was intended for the entire public and that they needed help in establishing it. When it was near time for the clinic to open, organizers placed notices in newspapers and everywhere else people might see them. They gave talks around the community to inform people of the new service.

Further steps are documented in clinic records. As the Shepherd's Hand ministry has evolved, its organizers have maintained a simple history from the program's pre-beginnings up through the present. The record of each step includes dates, which provide an overall

> **A running history can be helpful for any kind of public ministry, especially in the capacity-developing stages.**

picture of the time needed for various stages. Administrators can look back and compare results with initial goals, chart progress, see where they took a wrong turn, and learn from experience. A running history can be helpful for any kind of public ministry, especially in the capacity-developing stages. A log of a previously established ministry can also be used to start a new one since many of the steps are the same regardless of the ministry's content.

Learning from Mistakes

Shepherd's Hand is a good example of a ministry that is flexible and can change according to needs and resources. For example, in 2001 the clinic added two

73

new components to its offerings: a dental clinic and a prayer ministry.

According to Meg Erickson, clinic organizers had always hoped to include dental services. However, they moved gradually and took one step at a time. When they felt ready to expand into dentistry, they set up a trial program. That attempt ultimately proved unsuccessful due to unforeseen organizational problems. Of necessity, the dental clinic operated away from the church, in the offices of the volunteer dentists. After a time, says Erickson, it became obvious that there was too little communication back and forth between those offices and the clinic administrators.

Also, the dentists were not always clear on expectations of their services and ended up feeling overwhelmed by the program. Shepherd's Hand suspended dental care while it regrouped and reorganized. Erickson stresses that it's important to learn from mistakes—not to regard them as failures but as valuable lessons and learning experiences. On the second try, the dental clinic has operated much more smoothly. Changes have included training clinic volunteers to act as liaisons. They accompany a patient to the dentist's office and take care of all paperwork. The same volunteer accompanies the same patient each time, promoting consistency and familiarity.

The other new Shepherd's Hand addition is a prayer ministry directed by layperson Kris Teeples, who is trained in that skill. There was, she says, a desire among clinic volunteers to offer "more of a wholistic ministry" to patients, addressing needs beyond their specific physical problems. "We wanted to help meet their spiritual needs—but not in any way to impose on them," says Teeples. The challenge was, "How could we be available?" without making patients feel uncomfortable, since most patients are "outside of the church walls."

Teeples and Meg Erickson spent two years carefully thinking through and planning this new and sensitive ministry. Once again, they were flexible and open to learning from experience. For example, on a sign-in form for patients, they have been working with various ways of aking people if they wish to pray. They also retooled their volunteer training, stressing the importance of a volunteer's overall sensitivity toward a patient and his or her special needs.

The prayer ministry has its own mission statement that includes its scriptural foundation and the "three goals of a Shepherd's Hand Prayer Team Member." Teeples and another volunteer have been testing the ministry's methods, attending most every clinic session. She has decided that it's best simply to sit at tables with the patients as they wait to be seen, and to strike up general conversation in a natural and relaxed way. This approach often leads to opportunities for mnistry through listening and prayer.

Public and Private

Sometimes the volunteer and the patient may simply sit together in silence for awhile. Teeples emphasizes that the most important aspect of her training has been in "how to build relationship." She notes that, interestingly, the patients' most frequent prayer topic "is not their physical needs"; in fact, it's not for themselves at all. Rather, she says, "They may want to pray for problems a family member is having. One evening a mom wanted to pray for her children, who were getting into drugs."

The greatest challenge in the prayer ministry, according to Teeples, is "getting people to step over the comfort zone," that is, to learn to trust the listener and feel at ease in conversation. This is true for all aspects of ministry with strangers. Building trust is essential, but perhaps even more so with prayer since it is such a personal matter.

Part of the Shepherd's Hand Prayer Ministry includes volunteers' commitments to pray regularly at home for clinic patients. This is an intriguing type of public ministry. It does not occur "in" the public or even "with" the public, but, rather, behind the scenes in the privacy of the volunteer's own quiet prayer space. According to Kris Teeples, the experience of taking the ministry home and making it part of one's private life has the additional benefit of significantly enriching the volunteer's own spirituality. It integrates public and private in ways that nothing else can and thereby enhances both. It turns out that the "wholistic ministry approach" the parishioners desired has affected them as much as it has their public.

This is but one discovery in what Pastor John Bent calls the congregation's "growingopenness to possibilities and freedom regarding mission." Mission and ministry are dynamic processes. It is important once a ministry is established that its organizers remain flexible and responsive to changing possibilities the ministry itself might suggest. Such openness might lead to further creative interpretation of the congregation's mission. This process results in an ever-changing current ministry. It also results in new ways of thinking about that ministry or about ministry in general.

CHAPTER 7

"A BUNCH OF TROUBLEMAKERS"

OAKHURST PRESBYTERIAN CHURCH
DECATUR, GEORGIA

"That makes me think of another thing" was a sentence volleying like a Ping-Pong ball around a recent meeting of the Peace and Justice Committee at Oakhurst Presbyterian Church in Decatur, Georgia. Each new idea inspired several others. This committee illustrates the general atmosphere of encouragement and openness that pervades this congregation. Ideas for new public ministries or extensions of current programs never seem to stop. The congregation has a reputation in the Atlanta area for being involved in the most important public issues that arise. Members see themselves as what one parishioner affectionately calls "a bunch of troublemakers."

In addition to its reputation for cutting-edge public ministry, Oakhurst is a model of diversity—racial, economic, age, sexual orientation. Membership is about half black, half white, with a

> **Parishioners tend to attribute the congregation's growth to its pastor's dual emphasis on worship and public ministry, while the pastors give the credit for that emphasis to the parishioners.**

sprinkling of other ethnicities. There are less educated members and others with Ph.D.'s. There are a number of gay and lesbian members. Oakhurst appears as a case study of diversity in two books by Charles R. Foster: *We Are the Church Together: Cultural Diversity in Congregational Life*, with Theodore Brelsford (Trinity Press International), and an Alban Institute book, *Embracing Diversity: Leadership in Multicultural Congregations*. Consult those sources for a discussion of this other compelling aspect of the congregation's life (more information on these titles may be found in the Selected Resources section).

Oakhurst is a relatively small church, approaching 250 members. But 20 years ago it had only 80. Since the early 1980s, a clergy couple has served as pastors: the Reverend Gibson ("Nibs") Stroupe and the Reverend Caroline Leach. Parishioners tend to attribute the congregation's growth to its pastors' dual emphasis on worship and public ministry, while the pastors give the credit for that emphasis to the parishioners.

Oakhurst is not a wealthy church. In fact, until recently it was, according to one member, "economically challenged," and in many ways still is. A number of members, especially those from the immediate neighborhood, have trouble making ends meet. But they are generous with what they have and have learned to stretch a dollar beyond expected limits.

Changing Demographics

Decatur, with a population of around 19,000, borders Atlanta. According to Stroupe, for many years Decatur was home to lower middle-class working people, many of them African Americans who had jobs such as hotel maids or hospital aides. But in recent years, young white professionals have been moving into the area. As a result, property values have skyrocketed.

A number of problems have accompanied that rise. One is the rampant practice of manipulative or "predatory" lending, whose underlying purpose is to foreclose on a property or, at the very least, collect abnormally high loan interest. Commonly the home will be an older one owned by a senior citizen, most often an African American. The owner may have paid off most of the mortgage, but, because the home is old, it probably needs major repairs. Predatory lenders offer home-improvement loans or second mortgages

at exorbitant interest rates and those often include many hidden costs. They prey on people who have little knowledge of the home loan industry. Some of the homeowners have had credit problems in the past and might not qualify for a standard loan.

The loan marketers are highly aggressive, often going door to door in poorer neighborhoods convincing people they need to take out such a loan. Some of the lenders team up with high-cost, low-quality contractors who take on the repair work but often do a shoddy job or don't finish. Many borrowers run into trouble repaying the loans and may lose their homes, which can later be resold at the newer, higher property values.

This was happening to increasing numbers of people in Oakhurst's neighborhood and nearby. The congregation determined that it needed to become involved, and it chose a way consistent with its tradition: lobbying for state legislation to regulate the predatory lending industry. Associate Pastor

Caroline Leach has been involved with the congregation in many such efforts, and she stresses the importance of "going to where the power is" to try to effect change. The church's Peace and Justice Committee took on the task of educating the congregation and the community about the predatory lending problem and how they could help solve it.

According to Teresa Daub, then chair of the committee, their first move in early 2001 was to identify different kinds of people who might have information helpful to an education effort. They began to contact these people and to collect resources. Their next step was to plan a panel discussion and workshop focusing on the problem. They invited five speakers representing a broad spectrum of agencies and resources. These included a county commissioner, a lawyer from Atlanta Legal Aid, a representative from the Department of Housing and Urban Development, and an official from the county Human and Community Development Department, as well as an advocacy expert from the Presbytery of Greater Atlanta. (That denominational judicatory is very active in helping congregations develop plans and skills for this type of public ministry.)

The November 2001 workshop was a public event. According to Daub, approximately 60 percent of the participants were from the congregation and the remainder from the community. Many of the Oakhurst members do not live in the affected areas but wanted to learn how to lobby on behalf of those who do.

The experts talked about such matters as how to recognize predatory loan practices, how to read the fine print on a loan application, and how to protect one's credit. They discussed where people who have been targeted by unethical lenders can go for help.

The workshop also taught participants how to do effective advocacy and lobbying. For example, they learned, says Daub, that petitions and e-mail campaigns are far less effective than making phone calls to one's elected representatives. This is true even if that official is not on a committee that would deal specifically with the issue.

Participants also learned to use a government Web site to follow the deliberations on a particular bill as it makes its way through the state legislature. They learned that it is helpful to lobby not only as individuals but also as groups. And they learned that in addition to contacting their state officials, they could lobby businesspeople and write provocative letters to newspapers.

The workshop opened a variety of opportunities for follow-up, says Daub. The Peace and Justice Committee took on the further responsibility of tracking any relevant legislation, reporting on it to the congregation and the community, and organizing campaigns to keep pressing for stricter regulations. Committee members have continued to

> Petitions and e-mail campaigns
> are far less effective
> than making phone calls
> to one's elected representatives.

do all of this; for example, drafting a letter that writers could adapt on their own. If there is to be a vote on legislation, they will mobilize a widespread effort to notify all concerned. They have also joined and helped to organize demonstrations at the state capitol to express their views.

The Ex-mayor's Rummage

This kind of work requires an abundance of patience because its effects are rarely immediate; they tend to happen, if they do, in subtle increments. When taking on such a ministry it's important that participants have a realistic idea of what results may follow and when. Oakhurst is lucky in having among its members several who serve or have served in government, on regulatory commissions, community boards, or at health and other social service agencies. These individuals are familiar with the slow pace of such work, and they are able to describe for others the painstaking nature of such a commitment.

For example, Elizabeth Wilson, a longtime parishioner, has served as a Decatur City Council member and, in the early 1980s, as Decatur's mayor (the city's first woman and first African American to serve in that capacity). Prior to that she worked for a nonprofit health agency. She and others bring extremely useful knowledge and experience to the capacity-building stages of the congregation's ministries. Wilson is especially involved in one of Oakhurst's current public projects that is related to Decatur's changing demographics. As property values have gone up, so have taxes. Many older residents on fixed incomes, some of them Oakhurst members but by no means all, can no longer afford to pay taxes on homes they have owned for years.

In early 2001, Wilson invited a group of friends, mostly from church, to come for dinner and talk about the tax problem. Some of the people there were experiencing difficulty themselves; others were not but were sympathetic and motivated to help. According to Wilson, "We knew that legislation takes time, and were working on that separately." But they also knew that something immediate needed to be done for people who might lose their homes if they couldn't pay the taxes.

No one at the dinner had any significant money to put toward starting some sort of relief program. So Wilson suggested one of the time-honored ways in which churches have raised money: a rummage sale. At least, they reasoned, they and other Oakhurst members had plenty of rummage.

The group had only modest hopes for how much they might be able to raise—perhaps $500 to $1,000—but at least it would be a start. But they updated the rummage-sale concept, taking a number of steps to maximize their chances. Wilson asked a local merchant if the group could use his parking lot for the sale. This way there would be more display space, more room for parking, and the activity would be more visible than if it were held in the church. They also did more than the usual amount of publicity, announcing the event in a wide variety of places. When the "Junque Emporium" was over, the group had cleared more than $2,000.

Even that doesn't sound like much. But, as noted earlier, at Oakhurst ideas spread quickly and spawn new ones. Others at the church discussed how they could help in the tax relief project. Soon a number had pledged to donate their 2001 federal tax refunds to the effort. This generated notice and inspired others in the community to make donations. In the meantime, the "Junque Ladies of Decatur," as Wilson calls her group, put on another rummage sale—again far outdistancing their monetary goal.

The result was a quick accumulation of over $10,000—money that has gone directly to pay taxes for residents who could not afford to do so. The Oakhurst group channels the money through a community development corporation that works with the city to arrange payment plans for those most in need. There is a very specific set of qualifications that a recipient must demonstrate and Wilson, because of her government experience, was able to explore the details and draw up appropriate forms for the process. In less than a year, the group was able to help more than 20 of Decatur's neediest citizens pay their taxes and keep their homes.

In less than a year, the group was able to help more than 20 of Decatur's neediest citizens pay their taxes and keep their homes.

As noted, this was definitely not a situation of the rich helping the poor—far from it. For example, one of Wilson's original dinner guests, also an Oakhurst member, was Ethel Steverson, who has become an activist in the project. She works closely with Wilson in researching who might need tax help, informing them of the program, and processing all the red tape necessary to make it happen. Ironically, says Steverson, she originally attended the dinner because she herself was having tax trouble and thought the program might benefit her.

But, she laughs, "It hasn't happened that way." She has learned that "compared to other people, [I'm] doing well." What does that mean? "I'm able to eat," says Steverson, who is retired and has owned her home since 1973. To do some occasional upkeep and pay her taxes—along with new city fees occurring as a result of the real estate boom—"you rob Peter to pay Paul," she explains. "I just juggle." Realizing there were many people in greater need, she says, "I could not apply for the assistance with a straight face." Instead, she continues to juggle, and to spend her time and energy doing for others.

Interpreting the Text

Where does a congregation, especially a small one with modest resources, continue to find the energy and enthusiasm for social ministry projects that are providing so much benefit? Nibs Stroupe laughs as he answers: "In the Bible, of course."

When he was a young pastor just out of seminary, Stroupe thought that "social action was everything," and he confesses that his preaching was not always very biblically based. However, the more he became involved in public ministry, the more he realized that the impetus for a congregation to be able to take this kind of action "comes directly from the text. That's where the power is." In fact, according to Stroupe,

"Worship here sets a style for a public ministry." There is more of a connection between modern life and the Bible than many people realize, he argues. He and Leach have a commitment "to recapture the biblical text." It's a matter of learning to interpret those texts.

Worship at the church is dramatic and compelling. Biblical precepts come alive. Recently Stroupe and Leach presented a dialogue sermon about why the Bible's genealogies are not boring (really) and what they contribute to an understanding of Jesus' ministry. Using primarily Matthew's genealogy (Matt. 1:1-16) they discussed names in the list and asked who these people really were. Their point was that Jesus' ancestors included people (like King David) who were not always the most shining examples of virtue.

Also, some of those ancestors were not part of society's mainstream but lived at its margins, such as the foreigner Ruth or the prostitute Rahab. In relating this background to public ministry and explaining why it is important to understanding the importance of texts like the genealogies, they made the point that it is often at the "margins of society" where we need to look for meaning. Those margins are usually not within the church—they are outside, where the public is.

The Individual in the Public

Another strong message in the church's preaching and worship is the importance of performing public ministry in one's individual day-to-day life. An example is member David Schutten. Trained as a classroom teacher, Schutten says he has "been transformed" at Oakhurst. For him the encouragement toward public ministry was so effective that it changed his vocation.

Instead of teaching, Schutten is now president of the local teachers' union. He explains that "unions are weak in Georgia," and teachers lacked adequate

**It seems less like a church
of leaders and followers
than one of leaders and doers.**

representation in striving for fair wages and teaching conditions. So he "left teaching to do this more public thing." He "draws strength" from the congregation for the daily ministry he performs in the world. Nibs Stroupe points out that an important aspect of his own ministry is helping parishioners develop the self-confidence needed to realize fully their inherent talents.

Another example of individual public ministry is Suzette Gooch, a real estate agent who has practiced in the community for 18 years. Her ethical ways of doing business have generated a tradition of trust, especially compared with some of the methods that have accompanied the recent real estate boom.

In addition to dealing fairly with her clients on an individual basis, Gooch sits on boards of various organizations that are working, often with the church, to improve conditions in the community. She has served on various Oakhurst committees and is currently helping with the congregation's tax relief and reform projects.

She, too, credits the church's worship and congregational life with consistently renewing her energy for public work. This attitude is pervasive at Oakhurst. In fact, sometimes it's not easy to figure out who is responsible for what at this church. Everyone gives credit to everyone else: the members to the pastors, the pastors to the members, the members to each other. They are each other's models, inspirations, and biggest cheerleaders. It is possible to identify some leaders, but it seems less like a church of leaders and followers than, perhaps, one of leaders and doers. Actually, they all see themselves as followers: of a little child who leads them.

CHAPTER 8

MINISTRIES OF PRESENCE AND PRAYER

POST-SEPTEMBER 11,
NEW YORK CITY

It used to take the Reverend Amandus Derr 10 minutes to walk to work at Saint Peter's Lutheran Church in New York City. Now it can take him 30 to travel the six blocks from his apartment. Ever since September 11, 2001, says Derr, many walks have included stops on the street for conversations with people who want to talk about the devastating events. Some neighborhood residents recognize Derr as Saint Peter's pastor; other people see his clerical collar and don't care what denomination he represents. They simply seize the opportunity to talk to a clergyperson. Everyone in New York was deeply affected by the events, and people tend to look for—or find, perhaps unexpectedly—help where they are: where they live or work. So Derr now budgets extra time every day for unplanned conversations.

> Saint Peter's has various "publics";
> in fact, one could accurately call it
> a "public church." "Everything we
> do is a public ministry."

Saint Peter's has various "publics"; in fact, one could accurately call it a "public church." "Everything we do is public ministry," according to Derr. Saint Peter's is in the heart of Midtown Manhattan, away from the financial district where the Twin Towers were located, but similarly surrounded by office buildings that house corporations, law firms, publishers, and other commercial enterprises. It is also in an area that attracts many tourists, close to Rockefeller Center, Radio City Music Hall, and Fifth Avenue shopping.

The congregation has around 520 members, but there are always more worshipers than members at Sunday services. These are filled with tourists, out-of-town businesspeople, and New Yorkers who may or may not have their own regular place of worship. Since September 11, Saint Peter's has become even more of a public church in the ministries it offers addressing different aspects of the tragedy.

One of these offerings has been a series of educational programs to teach about Islam and its relationships with Christianity and Judaism. In this project Saint Peter's has worked with the Islamic Society of Mid-Manhattan as well as Central Synagogue, both of which are located nearby. Around the time of several holidays—Ramadan, Thanksgiving, Christmas, and Hanukkah—Saint Peter's and these partners held joint public worship and other events to symbolize their cooperation and mutual concern and respect.

Three years ago Saint Peter's opened a counseling center designed to serve primarily employees who work in the nearby office towers. The program began with one counselor working one day a week. But since

September 11, says Derr, "We've been buried." The center is now operating three days per week with two counselors. And there are more people to serve if it could expand further. The church's three full-time pastors are also spending more time in counseling. In fact, says Derr, sometimes employees in neighborhood offices will simply "call wanting to talk" on the phone.

Saint Peter's has another interesting "public." Its sanctuary is set below street level and open to the surrounding plaza and shopping complex. In addition to those attending a Sunday worship service, says Derr, "there are always 50 to 60 people who don't come down into the sanctuary, who may hang out in the balcony looking down or stand at the windows looking in." Even if they never enter the sanctuary, Derr figures the church is practicing ministry to these people as well. When he preaches, for example on a recent theme about being "a community of fearless people," he is talking to those in the balcony and outside too.

After the 11:00 A.M. service, the congregation holds a brunch that draws members and visitors alike. Previously, says Derr, average attendance was in the 50s. But "since September 11 it's never been under 80." It's not only the formal message from the pulpit that people seem to want and need, but the informal personal contact as well. Derr notes that recently the brunch has attracted a lot of young singles, people who have been drawn to New York for jobs but who may not yet have established any community and feel particularly lonely and vulnerable since the September events.

Another new public ministry for Saint Peter's has been its "September 11 Fund" for "the least, the last, and the lost." What particularly distinguishes this fundraising effort from others is the very direct way in which it reaches its beneficiaries. The congregation works with several organizations that have located the children of low-wage workers killed in the Trade Center disaster, some of them undocumented. Church volunteers find a relative or guardian for each child and set up funds in the child's name which begin flowing immediately with a minimum of red tape. The fund has attracted all kinds of contributions. For example, a Lutheran church in Arizona sent $13,000.

In this way Saint Peter's is filling another role as a "public congregation." It has become a symbol and rallying point for Lutherans around the world who want to help with the New York tragedy. Some would rather send donations to a specific congregation they've heard of instead of to a larger, more impersonal fund. Other churches have sent gifts such as candles accompanied by notes from children. In relationships like this, congregations can be said to form a kind of public for each other.

The same has happened with other congregations in New York, for example, Trinity Episcopal Church and its St. Paul Chapel, which are located very close to Ground Zero. As they became respite centers for rescue workers, they attracted attention and donations not just from other Episcopalians but from religious people everywhere. Sometimes a congregation chooses this type of symbolic role. In other cases, the role may be thrust upon a congregation. Either way, the challenge is in learning to wear the mantle effectively.

Adapting an Ancient Custom

Other congregations around the city have responded to September 11 with very different types of public ministries. One of the most affecting stories is that of Ohab Zedek Congregation, an Orthodox Jewish congregation on the upper west side of Manhattan, far from Ground Zero. Far, too, from the location of the primary outreach the congregation offered for eight months following the disaster. The location was the city morgue; the service performed was a continuous prayer vigil for bodies of disaster victims.

According to the congregation's rabbi, Allen Schwartz, the ritual is derived from the Jewish tradition of *shmira* ("to guard"): to hold a vigil over a body from the time of death until the time of burial. Jewish law requires that a dead body never be left alone. It also calls for burial within 24 hours, so normally such a vigil would be limited to that time. But the morgue was full of bodies and body parts that had not yet been identified and thus remained unburied. (According to Rabbi Schwartz a body part requires all the same care and attention that a whole body does.) So the members of the congregation organized a 24-hour, 7-day-a-week vigil to stand guard and pray at the morgue. Its most remarkable feature was how this congregation adapted a strictly Jewish tradition to embrace *all* victims of the devastation.

Many of Ohab Zedek's members serve in an ambulance corps. Despite the congregation's distance from Ground Zero, the corps's ambulances had been among the first to arrive at the disaster scene. This was because the corps requires volunteers to be sitting in a running ambulance ready to move at any time. According to Rabbi Schwartz, the ambulances had arrived before the second plane hit the Trade Center, and one of the vehicles was destroyed in that blast. "All that was left was a defibrillator," he says. That single artifact seems poignantly symbolic of how Ohab Zedek has been instrumental in reviving the city's heartbeat.

For 24 hours a day, in rotating four-hour shifts, a volunteer from the congregation or a participating group stood in a tent outside the morgue,

---

A defibrillator from a destroyed temple ambulance seems poignantly symbolic of how Ohab Zedek has been instrumental in reviving the city's heartbeat.

---

spending part of the time reciting prayers or psalms, and part of the time in religious study or silent contemplation. The project had official city approval, and the police who guarded the area issued a badge that each volunteer passed to the next when the shift changed. Because Ohab Zedek is an Orthodox congregation, its members cannot travel on the Sabbath except by walking. So they enlisted other Jews within walking distance of the site to fill the Sabbath hours. These included students at Stern College, the women's campus of Yeshiva University, which is located close to the morgue.

The vigil is a "ministry of presence," according to Armin Osgood, its lay organizer, reporting that hundreds of congregation members participated. Osgood was in charge of assigning the volunteers to their shifts and making sure there was always someone there. He never had to look for volunteers. In fact, he says, after people served one shift they would call back and say, 'I must do it again.'" Part of the reason, says Osgood, is that, in addition to fulfilling a religious obligation and providing a service for the victims' loved ones, the volunteers themselves discovered the vigil to be a remarkable spiritual experience.

In today's hectic society, explains Osgood, "everyone has the difficulty of finding spiritual time for yourself." Vigil participants told him that the time spent alone attending the bodies has "truly enhanced my spirituality." And although the experience took place for one individual at a time, sharing the experience among congregation members was "a demonstration of how a community comes together," he says.

Congregation members have also shared feelings Rabbi Schwartz describes from his own experience. One post-September 11 Friday evening, according to Schwartz, five city firefighters arrived at the close of Ohab Zedek's service to than the congregation for a donation to the Fire Department's fund for orphans. "The moment of their arrival, as they entered the synagogue was," according to Rabbi Schwartz, "one of the most moving moments I have had in my 17 years in the rabbinate."

The vigil ended on April 30, 2002, only after no more bodies were being recovered from the Trade Center site. According to Armin Osgood, that specific date was chosen because it marks an important time in the Hebrew calendar: "Lag b'omer" was the day a plague once stopped temporarily; it has always been regarded as a "half holiday during a period of mourning," he explains.

Responding to Joblessness

There have been countless secondary effects from the Trade Center disasters. One has been increasing unemployment in the New York metropolitan area. For example, shops, restaurants, and offices closed down or lost business, thus letting employees go. Tourism throughout the city dropped drastically so hotels, theaters, museums, and other enterprises have cut staff.

Judson Memorial Church, a congregation of the United Church of Christ and the American Baptist Churches, was already hosting an unemployment program that its organizers expanded in the wake of September 11. "The Employment Project," begun in 1994, addresses employment issues from a variety of perspectives that include study-conferences, lobbying, organizing, and publishing resources.

One of the project's regular features has been a support group for unemployed persons. Organizers use various means to publicize the group's availability, so participants come from all over the city. According to co-director Paul Chapman, after September 11 increasing numbers of people without jobs were in need of assistance that included not just help with finding information, but also emotional

93

support and an opportunity to talk about their experiences.

Because of the trauma that caused the current wave of unemployment, or at least worsened a trend already happening, Chapman and his colleagues realized that they needed to modify, tailor, and beef up their support group. "We expanded the focus . . . to consider survival questions in economic hard times—jobs, housing, debt relief, emergency food needs, transportation, health care," says Chapman.

Group leaders also came to realize the depth of emotional nourishment these jobless people needed, and that this holds true for well-trained, generally successful people along with those who have been less successful.

> A congregation can offer
> a place and opportunity
> for people to come together,
> not so much helping them directly
> as helping them to help each other.

Since September 11, according to Chapman, the meetings have included highly educated people who don't need to be taught how to reply to a job ad or to write a resume. What they need, he says, is "real emotional sustenance." Chapman does not see the group as providing pastoral counseling but as something else a congregation can do: offering a place and opportunity for people to come together, not so much helping them directly as helping them to help each other.

When new kinds of people started attending the support meetings after September 11, Chapman and his colleagues worried that the group might break down into smaller cliques according to class and economic distinctions. But that didn't happen at all. In fact, says Chapman, participants seem to find comfort in the fact that the job-loss issue cuts across economic strata. They have learned that, while the particularities of people's job problems may differ, the grief of unemployment is as much a public as a private problem. Says Chapman, group members learn that "there is strength in joining with others to face an uncertain future."

An Underserved Public

Of course, suburban congregations in the metropolitan area—New York, New Jersey, and Connecticut—were also deeply affected by the Trade Center events in a variety of ways. Many of the Tower victims were commuters who belonged to suburban congregations or were residents of their communities. These congregations have come up with numerous public responses. For example, Grace Episcopal Church in Nutley, New Jersey, initiated ministry to a public who has not received a lot of attention in all parts of the country: relatives and other loved ones of military personnel. These are not just military people serving in Afghanistan or on related missions, but those who could be sent overseas or into

some other dangerous situation at any time. In fact, loved ones of all service people are welcome to join the group.

Grace's rector, the Reverend Pamela Bakal, describes herself as "a yoga-vegetarian peacenik from the 1970s." Thus, when two of her sons decided to enlist in the military—one in the Marines, the other in the Army Reserve—she was surprised, though supportive. On September 11, "about two hours after the planes crashed into the Twin Towers," she says, one son telephoned that "he was anxious to be called up" to military duty. Suddenly, she was shocked into recognizing "the bigness of this reality. The safety of my child became a huge fear and anxiety." And she also realized that other families "must feel the same way, though nobody really talks about it."

Bakal determined that Grace Church could organize a support group for those families. She contacted experts in several fields and asked them to attend the group meetings and/or serve as resources. One of her first calls was to the Reverend Gerald Blackburn, an Episcopal priest and retired military chaplain (he now works at Episcopal Church headquarters in New York City as the director of military chaplaincies for the suffragan bishop for the armed forces, healthcare, and prison ministries). She also contacted the head of the Nutley Family Service Center, who is a mental-health professional. To notify the public of the meetings, she asked the Red Cross to send out flyers, alerted newspapers, and posted information on the Internet.

A diverse range of people started showing up—none of them Grace parishioners. They came from other churches or no church. In addition to family members, especially parents, several vets came, and they ended up playing an important role in helping the others understand what their own loved ones might be going through.

Of those attending the meetings, says Bakal, "One parent had a son in Afghanistan, another had a son in the Marines doing advanced desert training." Some had children leaving who couldn't say where they were going. Others had children in the military who were not in immediate danger but whose parents were worried anyway. According to Bakal, "many were uninformed" about military ways, military language, and what possibilities to expect. So, in addition to anxiety about physical danger, everyone felt confused and overwhelmed by the suddenness with which their loved ones' situations had changed.

Gerald Blackburn opened the first meeting by asking participants, "What are your main concerns?" He drew people out with larger questions like "Why does a young adult join the military?" The participants gained strength by sharing their experiences. And, according to Bakal, they particularly benefited by hearing from vets who had been in earlier conflicts, including World War II. "There were tears there for everybody," says Bakal. This public ministry has changed the way Bakal conducts regular congregational worship. For example, "the prayers of the people" have become a much more prominent part of every service, as members' concerns are probed more deeply. She and the congregation have become more sensitive to the vets among their membership, and in addition to praying for victims of terrorism now pray regularly "for all those who guard our safety." For a Veterans Day service, Bakal broke tradition by marching into the sanctuary carrying an American flag. She has changed her preaching to make it less theoretical and more accessible, asking herself, "What do people really need to hear?"

Bakal emphasizes that religious people "do not necessarily need to approve or agree with" the nation's military policies in order "to support the people involved." They are two different matters. The whole experience of starting the support group, says Bakal,

> **The prayers of the people have become a much more prominent part of every service, as members' concerns are probed more deeply.**

"has been humbling," and has opened the congregation to possibilities of other new ministries in the future. Gerald Blackburn thinks that a local congregation is definitely the right place to host such a ministry (although it might receive help from a national denomination or other body). According to Blackburn, "Everything happens right at the local level."

❖   ❖   ❖

All congregations who reached out following September 11—those in the New York area and elsewhere—have had an opportunity to redefine their ideas about public service. In addition to their embrace of a particular new ministry or way of serving the public, the act of exploring their own potential expanded their horizons. They also began to recognize a variety of needs they had never before considered, and to think about how their worship and congregational life might change through this new awareness. As a result of the tragedy, they have expanded the ways in which they relate to the world outside their doors.

A crisis can galvanize a congregation to examine its relations with its various publics. But these stories of publicly minded congregations indicate dramatically that innovation is alive and well as a regular part of life in any American congregations. The types of ministries described here are responses to very current problems, or new and creative responses to ongoing problems. And, in contrast to an earlier time when a congregation might have had one group of people interested in "social ministry" and another interested in "spirituality,"

these stories depict congregations where the two are intertwined inextricably.

This relationship is not always easy to express in worship, which is by nature part of a congregation's most internal life. In contrast, community ministry is an aspect of a congregation's external life. But these congregations are as creative in their worship as they are in their public outreach (attending worship was a crucial part of the research for profiles). These are not congregations of whom one might observe, for example, that their outreach is wonderful but their worship is boring, or that one outreach program is exciting but others are laconic.

This balance of worship and social action suggests that there is among these congregations an attitude and a process of openness and experimentation that both affects and grows from all aspects of a congregation's existence. Such a pervasive set of guidelines both undergirds and transcends everything the congregation does. More than just choosing the "right" public ministry, what goes into such a commitment is a result of a force much deeper and broader than one individual decision or program. All of these congregations are engaged in public service because of theological convictions that find expression in every other aspect of the membership's life together.

At the heart of the Hebrew and Christian Scriptures is the idea of the kingdom, or rule, or sovereignty of God. To be sure, that great idea developed over time, moving first from the more limited tribal notion of patriarchal times to the more universal understanding of the prophetic era. In post-exilic times, Israel found hope in a new, more eschatological picture—the kingdom might not be fully present now, but there would come a day, an end time, when all things would find their place and summation in God's complete rule. In the preaching of Jesus, the idea of the kingdom came closer—it is, paradoxically, both already and not yet. The kingdom is present in the mighty deeds of Jesus; it comes to life in the faith of disciples; and it will reach consummation one day in the future.

This is not the place to unravel all the permutations of so powerful, so fundamental, and so radical an idea. Rather, it is a place to make a connection. As I read *Public Offerings* I found myself returning again and again to this core belief. That was not what I expected. Instead, I brought to the book the expectation that I would learn some new things about the way congregations contribute to and shape public life. Indeed, that first expectation was met—and surpassed. Linda-Marie Delloff shows us a great deal about the kinds of public ministries emerging today and about the spiritual and practical resources required to create them. But these stories of 10 congregations' innovative ministries do more than teach about public ministry; they reveal how individual congregations extend God's

> In amazingly everyday ways congregations regularly find new ways to heal the world.

reign in the world—*today*. As the stories progress, she discloses one of the distinctive traits of congregations—their special character as early responders to the new needs of suffering people.

In amazingly everyday ways—such as putting food in a van and driving it to where homeless people in Washington, D.C. dwell, or creating a congregation-based health clinic for people lacking medical insurance in remote parts of Montana—congregations regularly find new ways to heal the world. This ministerial inventiveness is part of their essence. *Public Offerings* reveals congregational imagination at work both in creating innovative programs and in reading people's needs. Who comes up with these ideas—The Children's Center for Arts and Learning in Denver, an alternative high school for those whom the public schools fail to reach in the Back of the Yards of Chicago, or a lobbying program to stop predatory lending practices in a changing Atlanta neighborhood? Congregation members do. Often beginning in the heart of one determined and inspired leader, these public ministries grow and then change lives. As congregations step out and up in faith they learn to do new things, like applying for government funds or working city hall. At the same time, they also reshape traditional practices ranging from worship and confirmation instruction to prayer vigils and rummage sales.

The creativity and spirit of these 10 congregations are palpable on these pages. As one reads, one learns many practical things about public ministry. But as the stories unfold, more than techniques are learned. Readers are emboldened to say, "I never thought of that" or "Maybe we could do . . ."

For more than two decades, Linda-Marie Delloff and I have been regular conversation partners. She is a good friend, gifted writer, and keen-eyed reporter. We have talked at length about congregations and about the public difference they do—and must—make. With this book she seeks to move beyond our personal conversation to include many congregational leaders.

It is my hope that leaders of congregations of all sorts—Protestant, Catholic, and Jewish, urban, suburban, and rural, new and old, small and large, homogenous and diverse—will use *Public Offerings* to set off new conversations within their own faith communities. As they talk and then choose to act together, these conversation partners will see new opportunities and callings to love their neighbor. They will also see themselves and their congregations differently. And then in little and great ways they will write the latest acts in the unfolding drama of the kingdom of God.

JAMES P. WIND

The following list is not intended to be an exhaustive catalog of books, articles, organizations, Web sites, and other resources related to public ministry, but to provide a representative sampling of some of what is available to congregations to help them get started in community outreach and to maintain those ministries. Most of the annotations have been adapted from the Congregational Resource Guide Website(www.congregationalresources.org), a free, selective online resource guide developed by the Alban Institute and the Indianapolis Center for Congregations, and funded by Lilly Endowment Inc. Additional resource ideas may be found there. Another outstanding resource list is found in *Finding a New Voice: The Public Role of Mainline Protestantism* (more information below).

Books

Ammerman, Nancy T. *Congregation and Community*. New Brunswick, N.J.: Rutgers University Press, 1997.
The impact of social changes on more than 20 congregations in nine communities throughout the country are studied. With attention to such issues as changes in community racial composition, growing gay and lesbian populations, an influx of immigrant peoples, and economic dislocation, the book identifies four basic approaches that congregations take in response to those changes: persistence, relocation, adaptation, and innovation.

Ammerman, Nancy T., Jackson W. Carroll, Carl S. Dudley, and William McKinney, eds. *Studying Congregations: A New Handbook*. Nashville: Abingdon Press, 1998.
This handbook enables seminarians, clergy, academics, and congregational leaders to analyze the ministries, stories, and processes at work in congregations—sociologically, anthropologically, and demographically. This volume also helps pastors and lay leaders develop better plans and cultivate leadership skills as they examine churches in their environmental contexts.

Bos, A. David. *A Practical Guide to Community Ministry*. Louisville: Westminster John Knox Press, 1993.
David Bos has written this practical guide for congregations seeking to engage each other in serving their communities. Community ministry is unique in that it responds to both community and congregational needs. This book gives direction on assessing local community needs and on starting and developing a ministry.

Claman, Victor N., David Butler, and Jessica Boyatt. *Acting on Your Faith: Congregations Making a Difference*. Boston: Insights, Inc., 1994.
Victor Claman and his colleagues provide many brief sketches of congregations engaged in creative social ministry across the country. Examples range from providing sanctuary for

Central American refugees to teaching literacy in prisons. Readers are invited to consider a variety of arenas for social ministry in their congregations: food and shelters, health care, education, jobs, and more. The book includes "decision making worksheets," resources, and tips for getting started.

Devlin-Foltz, David, ed. *Finding a New Voice: The Public Role of Mainline Protestantism.* Washington, D.C.: The Aspen Institute, 2001.
This publication, based on the Public Role of Mainline Protestantism (PROMP) project, a research program of the Center for the Study of Religion at Princeton University, reflects broad collaboration and many voices, which resemble the mainline church's most typical—and often their best—public roles. Anchored by James P. Wind's central essay, "The Changing Voice of Mainline Protestantism," it features additional pieces by Missy Daniel, E. J. Dionne, Brad Verter, Robert Wuthnow, and others that provide wise and compassionate insights into how congregations must fulfill public roles in the 21st century. Completing the publication is an extensive resource list by Diana Butler Bass. A product of The Pew Charitable Trusts' initiative on Religious Communities and the American Public Square (RECAPS), it is distributed by the Alban Institute (www.alban.org).

Dudley, Carl S. *Basic Steps toward Community Ministry: Guidelines and Models in Action.* Bethesda, Md.: The Alban Institute, 1991.
Basic Steps toward Community Ministry suggests a set of working tools for developing community and social ministries. Detailing the start-up of 32 church-based projects from congregations of different sizes and persuasions, the book provides practical and simple guidelines to aid in naming the setting for ministry, the identity the congregation brings to the mission task, and the organizational pieces necessary for effective community ministry. *Basic Steps*, now out of print but available in libraries, has been replaced by a revised and updated edition, *Community Ministry* (below).

_____. *Community Ministry: New Challenges, Proven Steps to Faith-Based Initiatives.* Bethesda, Md.: The Alban Institute, 2002.

In this updated edition of his earlier *Basic Steps toward Community Ministry*, Carl Dudley guides congregational leaders in establishing and supporting community ministries, particularly in light of the post-9/11 world and governmental initiatives around faith-based social services. He looks at congregations as learning organizations, explores the relationship between faith formation and social action, presents examples of outstanding new ministries, and concludes with an updated resource list.

_____. *Next Steps in Community Ministry: Hands-On Leadership.* Bethesda, Md.: The Alban Institute, 1998.

The purpose of *Next Steps in Community Ministry* is to empower congregations to exercise their faith in developing community ministries. A follow-up to Dudley's *Basic Steps toward Community Ministry*, it charts the progress of 32 church-based community ministries after five years and identifies the motivation, organization, and resources most commonly found in effective community ministry.

Dudley, Carl S., and Nancy T. Ammerman. *Congregations in Transition: A Guide for Analyzing, Assessing, and Adapting in Changing Communities.* San Francisco: Jossey-Bass, 2002.

Dudley and Ammerman worked intensively with some 20 congregations to ground this workbook in real parish life. Here are practical exercises that will enable a congregation to notice its perceptions about what is and what may be. The work is in stages: understanding the congregation's roles and tasks in its community; understanding the history and meaning of people, resources, and processes; experimenting with reactions to options; and exploring the results of proposed actions.

Foster, Charles R. *Embracing Diversity: Leadership in Multicultural Congregations.* Bethesda, Md.: The Alban Institute, 1997.

Examining leadership dynamics in congregations that embrace racial and cultural diversity, Charles Foster invites readers to explore the dynamics of "difference" at work in the mission and leadership of their own congregations. While the book has been written for pastors and lay leaders of racially and culturally diverse congregations, it will also appeal to denominational officers and seminary students committed to equipping the congregations they serve for living hospitably in a racially and culturally diverse world.

_____. *We Are the Church Together: Cultural Diversity in Congregational Life.* Harrisburg, Pa.: Trinity Press International, 1996.

Gunderson, Gary. *Deeply Woven Roots: Improving the Quality of Life in Your Community.* Minneapolis: Fortress Press, 1997.
This book is actively visionary regarding the role that congregations can take in promoting the health of individuals in their communities and the health of the community as a whole. Although this book uses examples of many specific health ministries, it does not seek to give specific direction in establishing particular health ministries. It is practical in that it gives concrete suggestions on how a congregation may build a deeper, more transformative relationship to its community.

Harper, Nile, ed. *Urban Churches, Vital Signs: Beyond Charity toward Justice.* Grand Rapids, Mich.: Wm. B. Eerdmans, 1999.
Each of the 28 urban churches whose stories appear in this book has been rejuvenated into a community ministry center by launching social service and economic development projects and by taking political action to achieve justice for marginalized groups. Each story is accompanied by a list of learnings—such as the value of strong pastoral leadership, the power of local congregations to affect larger society, and the ways we can build on our church's history. Other urban churches will find inspiration in these stories, and even churches relatively unaffected by the problems of the inner city will find important suggestions for new ministry.

109

Jacobsen, Dennis A. *Doing Justice: Congregations and Community Organizing.* Minneapolis: Fortress Press, 2001.
A primer on the theology of congregation-based community organizing, *Doing Justice* covers such topics as the roles of power, money, and self-interest in organizations and explores how to build and sustain ministries that promote justice. It includes an index of organizations involved in congregation-based community organizing and a study guide for use by groups.

National Congress for Community Economic Development. *Restoring Broken Places and Rebuilding Communities: A Casebook on African American Church Involvement in Community Economic Development.* Washington, D.C.: NCCED, 1997.
Explores 12 case studies from African American churches that have undertaken significant ventures in community economic development around the country, including housing, small business development, capital formation, and commercial development. Includes informational and technical resources likely to be useful to church leaders seeking to initiate similar projects.

Oswald, Roy M., and Robert E. Friedrich, Jr. *Discerning Your Congregation's Future: A Strategic and Spiritual Approach.* Bethesda, Md.: The Alban Institute, 1996.
This incorporates the primary resources of discernment and prayer together with significant theoretical material—congregational size, systems, polarity management, congregational health and norms—into a useful and practical strategy for spiritual growth. The process is offered as a road map in which several activities and formats are suggested for each step, with the congregation, not the leader, at the center.

Queen, Edward L. II, ed. *Serving Those in Need: A Handbook for Managing Faith-Based Human Services Organizations.* San Francisco: Jossey-Bass, 2000.
Intended for both congregations and faith-based organizations (FBOs), this book explores their roles, relationships, and responsibilities in the provision of social services.

110

Included are such chapters as "Religion and the Emerging Context of Service Delivery," "Funding the Dream," and "Developing Financial Accountability and Controls."

Sherman, Amy L. *Restorers of Hope: Reaching the Poor in Your Community with Church-Based Ministries That Work.* Wheaton, Ill.: Crossway Books, 1997.
Restorers of Hope tells the stories of seven church-based or parachurch ministries that have helped transform communities and lives. It describes the programs and why they work, provides how-to advice to congregations wanting to begin their own ministries, and examines both the benefits of pitfalls of collaboration with government agencies.

Skjegstad, Joy. *Starting a Nonprofit at Your Church.* Bethesda, Md.: The Alban Institute, 2002.
Recognizing that many congregations are establishing church-based nonprofit organizations for community development, the author guides readers through the rationale and process for creating and maintaining a 501(c)3 nonprofit organization connected to a congregation. Included are chapters on assessment, defining mission, establishing accountability, fundraising, and evaluation, as well as an appendix on homelessness and housing issues by DeAnn Lancashire.

Thompson, George B. *Futuring Your Church: Finding Your Vision and Making It Work.* Cleveland: United Church Press, 1999.
Futuring Your Church presents a detailed process for clarifying congregational vision. Author George Thompson suggests forming teams to discover and interpret a congregation's heritage, context, and theological bearings, and use those to project a future vision of the congregation's calling. The book includes sample interview questions for discovering a congregation's heritage and theological bearings, resources for gathering demographic data, and clues for avoiding the pitfalls that often derail visioning processes. It also offers suggestions to help a team communicate its vision with the rest of the congregation.

Wilkes, Paul. *Excellent Catholic Parishes: The Guide to Best Places and Practices.* Mahwah, N.J.: Paulist Press, 2001.

Excellent Catholic Parishes presents sketches of eight Catholic parishes throughout the United States that have uniquely engaged the challenges facing them and have brought the gospel to life in an extraordinary way. These parishes invite the reader to new ways of looking at issues confronting the Church and their own parishes. Wilkes provides an index of "excellent parishes" throughout the States that "are a representative list of what is best in the local church."

_____. *Excellent Protestant Congregations: The Guide to Best Places and Practices.* Louisville: Westminster John Knox Press, 2001.

Excellent Protestant Congregations profiles nine Protestant congregations that exhibit "missional authenticity." These churches have looked at how to serve members and the community. With clear, often biblically based missions, they have tended to be risk-takers and self-starters who reach beyond their comfort zones. The book contains "A Points of Excellence" index and an index of "excellent congregations" by state and city.

112

Organizations

Cecil Williams GLIDE Community House (Glide Memorial UMC)
Glide serves the poor and disenfranchised in the San Francisco Bay Area and functions as a model for similar church-based programs around the country. Glide's 48 programs promote self-sufficiency and provide meals, AIDS testing, health care, women's programs, crisis intervention, basic services, literacy and computer training, job training and placement, and children, youth and family educational programs.

> Cecil Williams GLIDE Community House (Glide Memorial UMC)
> 330 Ellis St
> San Francisco, CA 94102
> info@glide.org
> www.glide.org

Center for Public Justice
The Center for Public Justice is a Christian civic education and policy research organization "committed to public service that responds to God's call to do justice in local, national, and international affairs." Its major policy studies include welfare reform and government and religious sector partnerships.

> Center for Public Justice
> P.O. Box 48368
> Washington, D.C. 20002-0368
> www.cpjustice.org

Center for Religion and Civic Culture
As a research unit of the University of Southern California, the Center for Religion and Civic Culture conducts research and analysis, provides documentation services, facilitates

conferences and consultations, and hosts a large Web site on public policy issues, faith-based human services and community organizing, and the civic role of religion in Southern California.

> Center for Religion and Civic Culture
> University of Southern California
> URC 106
> 835 W. 34th Street
> Los Angeles, CA 90089-0751
> (213) 740-8562
> crcc@usc.edu
> www.usc.edu/dept/LAS/religion_online

National Coalition for the Homeless
The National Coalition for the Homeless is a national advocacy network of homeless people, activists, and service providers who are committed to finding long-term solutions to homelessness. Its members raise public awareness and provide public education, policy advocacy, grassroots organizing, and technical assistance on hunger and homelessness, educational opportunities, addictions treatment and recovery support, and other issues.

> National Coalition for the Homeless
> 1012 14th Street, Suite 600
> Washington, D.C. 20005-3410
> (202) 737-6444
> nch@ari.net
> www.nationalhomeless.org

National Congress for Community Economic Development
As the association and advocate for the community-based development industry, The National Congress for Community Economic Development (NCCED) represents over 3,600

community development corporations (CDCs), which seek to create affordable housing and jobs through business and commercial development activities. The NCCED's services to the community development industry include public policy research, education, publications, conferences, and technical assistance.

National Congress for Community Economic Development
1030 15th Street, NW, Suite 325
Washington, D.C. 20005
(877) 44NCCED
(202) 289-9020
www.ncced.org

POLIS Center
The POLIS Center studies urban issues and provides research and information on churches and communities. The database of social indicators maintained by the center, and information about community assets and vulnerabilities are particularly useful.

POLIS Center
1200 Waterway Blvd, Suite 100
Indianapolis, IN 46202
(317) 274-2455
polis@iupui.edu
www.thepoliscenter.iupui.edu

Web Resources

Beliefnet Guide to Faith-Based Action
www.beliefnet.com/story/66/story_6608_1.html
Beliefnet, the "multifaith e-community" that covers religion in America, has put together a helpful guide to charitable choice in general and the Bush administration's faith-based initiative in particular. The site includes articles on the issues, reports on events and people, and links to major documents. Continually updated, this site is a good place to get an overview of the subject.

Faith-Based Involvement, Welfare Information Network
www.welfareinfo.org/faithbase.htm
The Welfare Information Network is a clearinghouse for information, policy analysis, and technical assistance on welfare reform. It has developed in-depth resources in many areas. The section on faith-based involvement is an excellent compendium of links to articles, papers, organizations, state programs, and service providers. This site is a good place to start when looking into the role of faith-based organizations in the delivery of social services.

Partnerships between Health Care and Faith-Based Organizations
National Center for Cultural Competence, 2001
www.georgetown.edu/research/gucdc/nccc/faith.pdf. (Adobe Acrobat required; see www.adobe.com for more information.)
Beginning with the observation that millions of Americans lack health insurance, this report argues for building safety nets through partnerships between health care and faith-based organizations. It outlines the goals of the federally funded Faith Partnership Initiative, which include building networks among faith communities to improve health, providing tools for collaborations between faith-based and health care organizations, and creating communication channels between faith communities and various stakeholders.

Presbyterian Peacemaking Program
Supporting churches in their commitment to peacemaking, the Presbyterian Peacemaking Program offers leadership development, conferences, and publications in a variety of areas: conflict management, community building, public policy, and international relations. Publications, including the booklets "Making a Difference in the Public Arena" and "Living Faithfully in the Public Square," may be ordered through its Web site.

> Presbyterian Peacemaking Program
> Presbyterian Church (U.S.A.)
> 100 Witherspoon Street
> Louisville, KY 40202-1396
> (800) 524-2612
> pds@ctr.pcusa.org
> www.pcusa.org/peacemaking

What's God Got to Do with the American Experiment?
www.brook.edu/dybdocroot/press/review/oldtoc.htm
This special issue of *Brookings Review* examines the public role of religion in the United States. The entire issue, which can be read online, contains material of interest to congregational leaders, but the section on faith-based social programs is a good introduction to the issues in the charitable choice discussion. The articles (in Adobe Acrobat format— see www.adobe.com for more information) include:

Cnaan, Ram. "Our Hidden Safety Net: Social and Community Work by Urban American Religious Congregations."
www.brook.edu/dybdocroot/press/review/spring99/ram.pdf
DiIulio, John J., Jr. "Supporting Black Churches: Faith, Outreach, and the Inner-City Poor."
www.brook.edu/dybdocroot/press/review/spring99/diiulio.pdf

117

Sider, Ronald J., and Heidi Rolland Unruh. "No Aid to Religion? Charitable Choice and the First Amendment."
www.brook.edu/dybdocroot/press/review/spring99/sider.pdf
Wilson, James Q. "Religion and Public Life: Moving Private Funds to Faith-Based Social Service Providers."
www.brook.edu/dybdocroot/press/review/spring99/Wilson.pdf